Since **2020**

HOT For This Month

Bagged Audi S3
An Audi on a budget that looks a Million Dollars

2

ATUK
Automotive Temptation UK Formed by a small group of mates in early 2019

14

Roush
Currently drive a 2008 Ford Mustang Roush, and also have an EP3 Type R J

18

Minnions
The lights, body kits, outrageous sound systems, and all the customization on every ride,

22

Voda Focus
The style I chose for my Focus is the silver and orange because I thought it was different to everyone else.

36

Its More Than a Passion for Cars

Next Months Special Feature

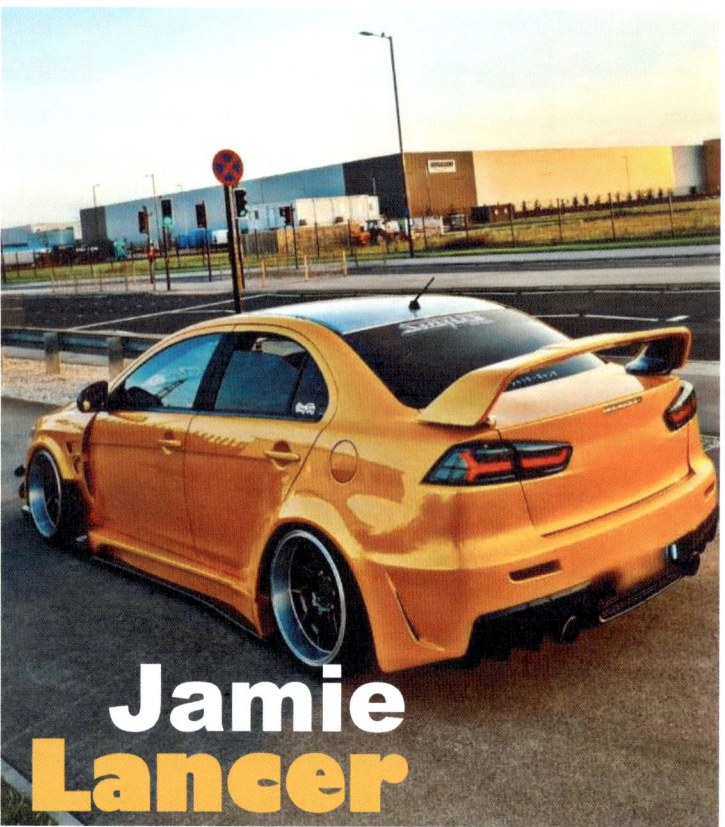

Mitsubishi Lancer
Jamie

I currently drive a Mitsubishi Lancer bought as an economical practical daily that's got out of hand and now is a wide bodied Evo rep or a D-evo.

My love for cars started at a young age with my uncles 1990 Astra GTE . Then grew from attending a Max Power show at Donny race course!

Growing up in the Max Power era has definitely moulded me as I've always wanted my cars to stand out from the crowd .. my lancer being the only wide bodied one in the UK and the only one to be painted in for Tangerine scream!

Instagram: @low.mpg

It's not been an easy road certainly down the performance road bolting on mods is one thing but then putting your pride and joy into the hands of a mapper can be a minefield .. I'd strongly recommend doing your homework before doing so.
She's currently running 200 Bhp but with the hardware under the bonnet 240-250 Bhp is possible with more dyno time.

A lot of the work I have mostly done myself with help from friends the full respray and smoothing out the body work was done by my mate Pav and his team at **@driven_custom_vehicles.** Fitting the kit initially and a few other bits my mate Didzis massively helped me with thankfully.

My first motor was a far cry from then lancer. it was my dad's 5 door 1.4 206! Soon as I started working I banged 17inch wolf race rims on and the usual Halfords trinkets! Wasn't long before it was upside down in a field ha-ha!

As far as what does the future hold for the lancer. I'm not really sure. I wouldn't ever say it's finished. if it was that means I'd be bored of it and want to sell it... which wouldn't make sense as I'd never get back what I spent !You'll see me at the main shows about the country with the **@mitsubishi_lancer_UK** group.. a cracking bunch of lads a lasses always a top outing when we get together. Looking forward to Trax, Japfest this year !

Author: Carla De Freitas

Phil Griffith's
Bagged Audi S3 8P

So, It all started riding off road bikes when I was 6 years old, my father was massively into his motorbikes and was a huge collector of the Kawasaki z900, hidden within the garage was his pride and joy, a forever car project, collecting dust, rust you name it, my dad's e30, every day after school I used to get the Emery cloth out the cupboard and try to take back the rust not knowing it would come straight back.

As time went on, the e30 got an engine rebuild by my dad, I tagged along helping him after school. Since then I couldn't take my hands off anything mechanical, then went onto rebuilding my kx125's engine at the age of 13. That's how my passion for cars comes from, and then the discovery of the legendary fast and furious, then ... all hell broke loose.

Instagram: @PH11_WTF

Engine & exterior:

Stage 2+ carried out by Awesome GTI 390hp
All supporting mods ...
Airlift v2 management with performance struts
H&R front and rear roll bars
Every single bush is Polly bushed including engine mounts BBS 19" CH-R Wheels Falken fk510 all-round RS3 front grille
Rs3 diffuser
RS3 spoiler
RS3 rear bumper
Maxton splitter & spoiler extension
Magna rear diffuser extension

Interior:

RS3 wing back seats
RS6 carbon steering wheel
R8 carbon trims
Rear bench removal
Rear custom boot build
Custom roll cage

Photographer
Facebook: **untypicalmediauk**
Instagram: **@untypical_media**

The car scene for me takes me away from what's happening in the background, being around chilled vibes, sick cars, and amazing people, what's not to love about it? From meeting new people to discovering crazy builds every car meet/show I attend still to this day amazes me.

Knowing there are all these hidden gems stored away in someone's garage, and they only get brought out when the car shows are running. Without being a car enthuses how else would you expect to see these machines?

I drive an Audi S3 8P Old but gold, seems like nowadays everyone is starting to forget about these things, before I got this I had plans to build a fast show car, and had my eyes set on a golf R, this was to my high end of my budget and would struggle to do the modifications I wanted to unless I went on finance. "Sod that, get something older and make it look better than a Golf R "that's what my thoughts were. Then I started looking into the RS3 8P but again couldn't afford it unless finance.

This is where the s3 came in, Buy a cheap – ish s3 make it my show car then eventually make it into a RS3, which is the long term goal! Currently engine wise I'm at stage 2+ running

390hp with all the supporting mods, also have a stage 3 turbo and manifold on order! Furthermore, how do I get in shows nowadays? Seems like all I need is bags and some flashy wheels … Well I wanted to do it a bit different as I had my car always set up for track use. Why not go down a "track car/show car look

The build began..

Started off with the engine mods, and suspension and wheels then eventually realised I wanted air ride as I wasn't getting into the shows, so that's what I did, followed the band wagon and got airlift v2 management along with my legendary BBS CHR wheels, no 3 splits round here .. once I did that it just looked like any other car on bags so then I needed do something to stand out from the crowd.

So I found a rusty universal roll cage on the internet that needed re-welding spraying etc. me and the lads at work fabricated it so it actually fitted my car resprayed it and tried to bolt it in not realising it won't fit as I had back seats, so that's where the interior came in, again needed to stand out from the old "bag and wheel build" so that's when I redid the interior.

RS3 wing backs, RS6 carbon steering wheel, carbon R8 trims, took the rear seats out and rebuilt the whole interior on my mates front garden, MDF bit of curtain I found online, manual labour and £100 later I had myself a one of a kind boot build. We resprayed it in a big cupboard my mates had in his garden.

A Dream Car Built on a Budget

My cars not the best looking VAG out there I know, but when you're working with a budget and trying NOT to get yourself into debt, you work with what you've got, that's what makes my Audi unique from the rest, what you see is what I have done with my own hands apart from the important stuff.

shout outs @awsome GTI, for the engine work and @airtekautomotive for the bag install.

Also my support from the groups I rep, @downlowoffical, @vagsocity, @dunkingbuscuit .

And the BOYS for the help in grafting!

Future car? RS3 swapped S3.

Future plans? stage 3 next couple of weeks should see 430 plus, but then like I say I can't afford a RS3 so I'm going to make my S3 into one, mark my word 700hp inbound baby.

Author: Paul Doherty

Rogue Static

Formed by a small group of mates in early 2019, Automotive Temptation UK set out to attack the UK car scene in a new and exciting way. By focusing on creating an equal platform for brands, clubs, enthusiasts and business to connect via social media platforms, it wasn't long before the name took off. By hosting a range of events throughout 2019, including collaboration meets with local clubs, the team soon began to expand quickly, making lots of exciting connections.

ATUK covered all areas of the automotive scene, everything from Motorsport to organised shows. Towards the end of 2019, ATUK decided to expand further, and explore the possibility of providing media, and documenting the scene from a first person perspective. With a lot of tedious planning and investment, the ATUK media team was formed. This allowed the group to not only provide constant photography at events, but to start up their YouTube channel.

Since the start of the YouTube channel, ATUK has worked with a range of companies from around the UK, to produce new and exciting videos. The main video series 'ATUK Tours' comprises members of the team, vlogging at local events, and showing their perspective, while including a range of montages and compilations.

Unfortunately due to the COVID-19 pandemic, operations were halted in order to protect both the team, and members of the public. As the UK lock down conditions continue to ease, ATUK is slowly beginning to make a comeback, in a way that ensures everyone is safe, but continues to enjoy the passion we all share.

As time goes on, ATUK only plans on aggressive expansion, with plans to announce some amazing projects over 2020/2021. The team will be continuing to attend events such as motor sport events, street meets, organised shows and media events. The team will also continue to work with companies from around the UK, to provide media, products and services to their followers.

You can find out more about Automotive Temptation UK over on their social media platforms:

Facebook: Automotive Temptation

UK Facebook group: ATUK

Community Instagram: @Autotuk

Website: Atukclub.com

YouTube: Automotive Temptation UK

We are always looking for new and exciting people to join us on our journey, contact us today to join the movement!

For business enquiries, contact us on - info@atukclub.com

A Northwest based car community for ALL types of car enthusiast.

From your daily project to a show stopper you will find yourself welcome right here with us.

Over the last 18 months of progression, our small community has exceed our thoughts,

From a few friends to a massive family of members spread out across the nation.

Monthly events to raise funds and awareness for our hand picked, deserving charity

Drive outs, track days and cars and coffee events all planned for our valued members

We are a family orientated car group, so our hosted and collaboration events are safer due to promoting only STATIC events,

We work with some of the greatest, like minded people from other groups to bring something new for everyone no matter what background, everyone is welcomed and treated like family.

We will be holding track specific events letting you unwind and release the animal inside too.

Our main goals are to work with our local communities and groups to provide legal, safe events for everyone,

ALL our merchandise profits and entry fees raised by our events go directly to our charity, SSAFA the armed forces charity,

@roguestatic

Author: Paul Doherty

Keiran
Subaru Impreza WRX300 No.158
Instagram: @Scooby_Wrx300

This is my Subaru Impreza WRX300 No.158 of a limited run of 300 cars.
My passion for cars probably started in my early teens, I was always collecting magazines such as Max Power, Fast Car and Redline as they always came with free stickers (and as a teen you wanted to see some boobies lol) then came Fast and the Furious and made the car scene even bigger, Once me and my friends left school everyone started buying their first car and driving about every hour of the day, after this I was hooked on cars and began attending the Max Power shows,

My first car that I purchased was a Peugeot 106 XSI, for a little 1.4 engine this car certainly had a fight in him, after this I had a couple of MK3 Escorts in which one was a cabriolet with a Fibreglass Cosworth body kit and bonnet and sprayed Cadburys' metallic purple, You couldn't miss me lol, from there I moved around from hatchbacks to saloons and bought my first Subaru Impreza which was a 1998 UK2000.

I was so excited as this was my first turbo'd car and also AWD, due to the excitement I rushed into buying it and soon realized what I had got into, after a few repairs and the birth of my first child it was decided that the Subaru was to go and make room for a family car, this being a Vauxhall Insignia CDTI SRI VX-Line, a brilliant family car but had no fun factor anywhere, after one year of ownership I knew I needed another Subaru in my life so here we are, I purchased the car 2 years ago with only a few engine modifications, an STI spoiler and side skirts, the rest of the car was standard, I knew straight away that this car was sticking around for a while so I started to plan the modifications, the first thing I did was clean up the engine and replace some of the covers and replace some of the tired pipes and wires.

After this I moved onto the bodywork and wheels & Suspension. The first set of wheels I bought were some Gold OZ Superleggera that really set the car of bringing back the traditional Blue and Gold theme, then came the suspension which I opted for fully adjustable coil overs as I had a couple of issues with the standard shocks, not long went by and after a few more little changes the car was starting to look how I wanted it.

Then came the moment I wanted to change it up, so away with the traditional gold wheels and along came some Rally White Fifteen52 Turbomac, then I decided I wanted to be a bit different so opted for pink detailing on the car, my favourite modification to the car is my front splitter, my friend Alex had cut and fitted it but I then choose to fiberglass it to the original splitter making it a complete one off splitter, below you will see its current spec list,

Being the WRX300 this came with a few upgrades being the Prodrive performance package, blue alcantara Subaru world rally team seats as well as some other additions/changes,

Future plans for the car full car livery (not Subaru graphics) and after that will be moving inside to the interior but you will need to follow my Instagram if you want to see it,

I love the car scene and have met some really interesting people and cars, the best thing I can take away from all of this is the friendships that have been made along the way,

The most enjoyable times are when we all meet together whether it's at a local meet or at a big show somewhere around the country, if you see me at a show/meet please come and say hello and if you spot my car don't be scared to tag me,

Mod/spec list:

VF35 Turbo
Sti Pink Injectors
Sti Intercooler
Sti Inlet Manifold
RCM induction kit
Walbro 255lph fuel pump
3 port boost solenoid
Decat Up Pipe
Decat 3" Turbo back Exhaust
Exedy Stage 1 organic clutch
Exedy lightweight flywheel
Blitz Dump Valve
Remapped by Duncan Graham @334bhp Mishimoto rad and header tank caps
Mishimoto radiator brackets
Zero Sports induction pipe
Blue Silicone intake pipe
Blue Sti silicone hoses
Badass Performance Aux belt,
slam panel & battery cover painted Magenta
Pink Fuse box and Maf cover painted Magenta
Pink Adjustable coil overs
Fifteen52 Turbomac's 18" 9.5j

Inertia:

Sony CD player with Blue tooth and Voice control, 12" sub and Amp
Boost, oil temp and oil pressure gauges

Exterior:

STI spoiler
STI side skirts
STI Bonnet scoop
WRC style roof spoiler
Angel Eye Headlights Fog covers
Air feed through fog cover
Custom made front splitter
Rear bumper spats Rear diffuser
Vortex roof fins
Perrin wing stiffi's
Scooby World Mud-flaps
Tinted windows

Author: **Paul Doherty**

My name is Nick Cosentino and I currently work as a Software Engineering Manager.
I've spent the last 8 years of my life helping create some of the world's leading digital forensics software. When I'm not working, I'm at the gym, with my pups, or out and about with the car!

Ignantt is a *2012 Audi TT RS*, or what's left of one. I've really loved European cars once I switched over to them, and coming from a small BMW 135, I wanted another car that was small with a bit more kick to it. The TT RS was unique with it's 5-cylinder engine and uncommon in North America, which made it appealing for me. It was my first move into the Audi family, and I certainly fell in love as soon as I had the opportunity to drive it.

What got me into the car scene? Let's just say it was all accidental. I never thought I would have spent this much of my life invested into cars, the car scene, and meeting all of the people both locally and internationally just from cars.

When I purchased my TT RS, I knew before I bought it that I wanted it in matte red. I was set on that! I didn't care what colour the car came as because it was going to be wrapped matte red as soon as I bought it. The wrap shop asked if they could show off the car at a car show when it was complete, and I thought that would be an awesome way to help give back for the work they were doing.

I guess it's not right to say "and it was all downhill from there", but the phrase fits in terms of momentum. From that first car show the itch needed to be scratched. Wheels. Suspension... it was sort of game over really. Getting to learn and be part of the culture was a really awesome experience.

I can't take credit for a lot of the work that's been done on the vehicle, just a lot of the direction that it's taken. People that are close to me know that the past few years of working with this car have been a living nightmare for me facing a mid-season engine blow-up, the entire next season being lost to a delay in parts being fabricated, and more recently having to fully rebuild the engine a second time. This will be almost the third full season in a row that I lose out in driving this car and I think that it's a sign that we're done with it after it's finished up. At some point it's more of a stress than it is something to enjoy, and I think about 2 years ago is when I passed that threshold.

I've made it my rule to only speak positively about experiences and omit sharing negative experiences as to not play a public blame game. I don't think that's fair for anyone!

Special Thanks To:

'JP Powder Coating' - (@jppowdercoating)
'Berlin Klassik' - (@berlin_klassik)
'Chopshop' - (@chopshoptgsc)
'Incurve Wheels' - (@incurve)
'Lavigne Motorsports' - (@lavignemotorsports) 'Limitless Wraps' - (@limitlesswraps)
'Niko Signs' - (@nikosigns)
'LinkMedia.co Photographers' (linkmedia.co)

I had *Chopshop* based near Hamilton/Cambridge area in Ontario do a lot of the work on my vehicle. The owner Kevin was always able to give me a lot of support with getting things put together. He's known for putting together amazing air set-ups, so I was fortunate enough to have him on board to get mine done up.

I've had a local wrap shop called *'Limitless Wraps'* help tremendously with the vinyl, and at different points in time the wrappers there have helped me out when operating under different names. They've always come in clutch for me. Another local shop called *'Niko Signs'* and *'Grafx'* has also helped out when I've needed it, so I really appreciate both these shops being there for me.

'JP Powder Coating' has done all of my powder coating work and certainly added some awesome touches to the car. When people saw the purple block or got a chance to see the custom two-tone brakes up front that's where they start to realize the detailed effort put into the car.

More recently *'Lavigne Motorsports'* is assisting with rebuilding the engine. The owner Eric has been a great help with explaining what's going on as the rebuild progress has commenced.

The Audi was not my first car in fact, my first car was a 2003 Chrysler Intrepid however, the Audi is the first one I have probably spent too much money on!

I wouldn't consider the car finished yet! Maintenance and colour changes will happen after this. I haven't been able to truly enjoy this car for almost 3 years now. There's too much time missing now and I can't get it back. I'd like to just enjoy what I have once it's running properly again.

I've done quite well at car shows in Ontario. The car generally catches a ton of attention because of the bright exterior, but the trunk setup is generally what really gets people when they come up close to check it out.

The past few years I haven't been able to enter many shows because of the downtime with the car.

What's my dream car? Question of all times!

There are plenty of nice cars I'd love to have for different reasons.
Next purchase will be something "spooky", but I'll be saving up for quite some time still.
I'll leave it at that!

My Full Spec List can be found on my Online Feature
WWW.STANCEAUTO.CO.UK

Author: Carla De Freitas

Jake Arnell — Audi A4 b6 1.8t Bex Sport Quattro

Instagram - @bluebay_b6

Hi I'm Jake Arnell 31 years of age , I work in the dockyard in Portsmouth UK

I'm a family man, wife and 3 kids, I haven't been in the car scene that much I've done my car for myself, I've loved modified cars since a young age and the wife (Mandy Arnell) told me if I love modified cars it's about time I did something to mine.

I picked my car as there used to be a standard one with a set of lemans that I fell in love with so I had to get myself one.

Exterior:
Complete respray in Danish blue
Bola B1 wheels
Airlift proformance V2
Oettinger front end
S4 rear end
Side skirt extensions
Brembo 18z 6pots
Flared arches + 1.5" widened at the front
to line up with the bumper

Interior:

JHM Short shifter
Complete change from grey to black
Corsa vxr Recaro wingbacks customised to
fit (rears painted to match the car)
Car on center console with sides retrimmed
in alcantara with diamond stitching
Glove box + steering rack cover + handbrake
retrimmed in alcantara with diamond stitching Handbrake
carbon fiber button
Rs4 gear knob
TT flat bottom steering wheel
Boost, oil temp and oil pressure gauges in custom
made vent
Retrofit ambient light in blue to over head lights
front and rear + door handles, all vent lights changes
from red to blue
Turbo timer with voltage meter
S4 clocks
Carbon trim
The full respray was done by *@brownsidecustoms* and myself

Engine:

Precision turbo Gt3076r T3
Atp 3 exhaust manifold
Tial external wastegate
Screamer pipe
Mishimoto big fmic
Baileys b.o.v
Induction kit (relocated intake) Custom downpipe
Milltek cat back exhaust non resonated

Everything on the car I have done/fitted myself or at least helped and got my hands dirty mostly outside my flat from fitting the airlift to swapping out the turbo all road side.

Up and coming plans are first to retune currently running 260hp on the last turbo a retune should push to 350hp tlll rods and fuel pump are upgraded.

Retrim rest of interior, rear just needs diamond stitching as already alcantara doors and sets, front needs to be trimmed with alcantara + diamond stitched.

Then to get the wingbacks retrimmed to match the rest.

Custom make a new gator

Carbon RS4 gear knob and steering wheel and just add carbon where I see fit so hopefully most of it.

I am admin of a club called @Audib6ix few of us wanted a club where everyone respects each other and our passion for the b6 model of the A4.

When I was younger I always wanted a Golf mk1 with a Hayabusa engine and being a bit older I started getting a soft spot for the Nissan silvia s15 sprc R but having kids that one slipped away from me.

Author: **Paul Doherty**

MAT - VAUXHALL ASTRA 1.9 SRI

The Vauxhall Astra was not my first car, in fact, my first car was a Corsa B that my nan gave me after I passed my test and yes, I do still own the Corsa B and it is back on the road as my daily.

At the current time, I am not doing stuff to the car, I work full time for the CO-OP as a team leader whilst also being a professional boxer and a dad to three beautiful kids!

*I would say I probably got into the car scene when I was 14 and collected '**Max Power**' magazines and watching 'the **Fast and the Furious**' movies*

The Vauxhall Astra was not my first car, in fact, my first car was a Corsa B that my nan gave me after I passed my test and yes, I do still own the Corsa B and it is back on the road as my daily.

Here is my MK5 Vauxhall Astra 1.9sri also known to everyone as 'Tigger'.

So let's get onto the stuff you really want to know about my Astra!

I purchased the Astra completely standard 4 and a half years ago with absolutely no intentions on keeping it as it was mainly a family car to get around, however, I really started loving it so I started doing bits to is such as, changing the wheel colour, lowering it and window tints then decided I really wanted to make it unique, different and stand out from the crowd. From this, I got my partner to start drawing the car and doing things on it like bumper colours etc. I can't draw so the choice of the Orange came from that and let's be honest, how many Orange Astras do you actually see?

So the story began there with the Orange Astra, it is now my second year doing shows! My close mate's Ant and Emily, who we tend to do all the car shows together told me to bring a Teddy to stick in the engine bay so the only teddy I had was my daughter's Tigger!

*Tigger would be present at every show and everyone who would see him would say '**Look it's Tigger the Astra**' and that's where it all began properly.*

FULL SPEC LIST

EXTERIOR:

One of a kind orange paint
Vxr bumper
The lower bumper is the Kuro carbon with the cm composite splitter
XP rear bumper with custom defuser
Just finished having a custom rear lower cm composite splitter made
Side skirts extensions also just being fitted
We have the 12mm bonnet raisers in with the bonnet vents

INTERIOR:

Vxr Ricardo full leather seats
Full dash smd conversion
Three gauge set up oil boost and volts
Carbon dipped steering wheel plastics Black and orange dash
Pioneer app radio 3

ENGINE:

1.9sri engine.
Hybrid 1756 turbo running 2bar boost.
Custom intercooler and pipework. 80mm MAF.
Air filter.
EGR delete and blanked.
Dpf delete.
Swirl flaps welded.
Custom painted engine cover.
2.5 downpipe into 2.5 straight through into cobra duel exit.
Running 225bhp.
350ft toque.

SUSPENSION:

V2 air ride customised to slam properly With boot build but currently being redone to show standards

FRONT LIGHTS:

Bi-Xenon duel projects light output high and low beam
Colour chasing halos in both lights plus fogs plus engine bay and intercooler
Audi style indicates /Drl strips too

ALLOYS: B1 bola in shadow chrome

REAR LIGHTS:

Fully one of a kind custom build rear style likes 1/1 made just for my Astra with blue ghotz system's standard drive mode n show mode witch is insane BTW both lights are fully program-controlled from my phone

All made by monkey wrench bespoke

All bodywork is looked after by my sponsorship with **4k detailing** providing me with the good to protect the paint wheels etc.

All paint is covered by my sponsorship with **JS Customs** in Leeds helping me keep Tigger in top-notch condition for the shows.

WE ARE STILL BUILDING THE CAR

The list to still goes on as follows:

Audio build /Custom build
New alloys
New headlight builds with bigger spec
New seats
Harness
Harness bar
And possibly an engine conversion to the z20 let providing I don't choose to go bigger derv power

Club wise I am in quite a few of them, the main one which I spend the majority of my time with is 'Vauxhall Modified', Griffin Gang and a few others too.

THE SHOWS I TEND TO HIT EVERY YEAR ARE:

Fast show
Vauxhall show
Mods nats
Usc
And Trax

But of course, I wanna hit more of them hopefully next season I can get to twice as many!

If I was able to own any other car it would have to be the R24 GTR 2.5 Twin Turbo, I have always loved this car from a young age.

Thank you for reading my article and don't forget to follow my build on Instagram.
@Tigger_sri_mat

Mat

Author: Andz Stinton

Ford Focus ST
Paul Drinkwater

Instagram: @voda_focus_st3

My name is Paul aged 42 from Portsmouth. I've got a fiance and two sons. I bought my ST 3 years ago and started modifying it straight away.

My dad did banger racing for about 10 years when I was a kid, I used to love going and watching all the cars going round and getting smashed up. When dad used to come back with the car all wrecked I used to sit in it and pretend I was the driver. He used to buy me the banger racing stickers and I would collect them.

I've always wanted a Ford ST from the minute I saw one. I knew I wanted that. My dad always had Fords so I knew my car had to be a Ford. When my sister's boyfriend got a Ford Focus ST in blue I knew I had to get one too.

I've met many new people through the car scene, going to car shows and seeing stunning cars.

They love sitting in my car and showing it off pretending to drive it too. I'm part of a car club EFS UK (Elite Ford Society) run by Rich Horton, and we convoy to car meets all over the country.

We also meet up socially to chat about cars, and everyone helps each other out. We are always looking for new member's to grow the group!

The style I chose for my Focus is the silver and orange because I thought it was different to everyone else. Decals were done by Panther modz, where I started with the ST Vodafone decal, which I am the only person to have, and just went on from there.

I am due to have the roof wrapped in gloss black with decals at the end of August. I think the bright colours make the car stand out, as well as the loud exhaust. I came second in the rev off at ford fair 2019.

Spec List:

RS Clutch
Milltek ultimate exhaust Block mod
20/40 lowering springs
K&N air filter
RS ECU holder
Strut brace bar
Stage two air tec intercooler
Uprated discs
Airtec recirc valve
Turbo smart wastegate actuator

5-inch tips RS spoiler

Zunsport lower grill TRC front splitter
19-inch TSW vale alloys

Author: Paul Doherty

Instagram: @the_purple_dildo

THE PURPLE DILDO

Ian - 2008 Ford Mustang Roush

My name's Ian, I'm a 38 year old I.T nerd currently living in the magical town of Northampton where hopes & dreams go to die!

Currently drive a 2008 Ford Mustang Roush, and also have an EP3 Type R J

I've been into modified cars since I could drive, god I miss the Max Power days! First car was a Nova SR, cost me £600 to buy, spent every penny on it, and that truly gave me the modifying bug! Since then I've been involved in the majority of "scenes" from jap (owned 350z, Pulsar GTiR, Civic), VW (owned classic bug), yank (owned numerous muscle cars from '66 Mustang, '72 Nova, Camaro, Chevy 3100, and current Mustang).

My dad was a massive petrol head, and he was always there to help advise/fix things when I blew them up (including 3 engines on the Nova!).

So onto the car…

It's a 2008 Ford Mustang Stage 1 Roush – the stage 1 is mostly body styling e.g Roush body kit, high performance exhaust etc. I picked this as you simply can't beat the sound of V8 muscle, and I wasn't a fan of the new shape S550 Mustangs.

If the insta tag didn't give it away I don't take things too seriously, and like to have a laugh. Indeed the tag, and car nickname came round because friends decided to take the piss when I had the car initially wrapped in a purple/fuchsia colour, and they said it looked like a dildo!

I bought the car approximately 2 years ago, and it was pretty much standard. Quickly got to work by adding ordering the trufiber hood & Raxiom Headlights, the import fees alone cost more than the actual items!! I then added some 20" rims, lowering springs, and had it wrapped. Unfortunately the initial wrap was absolutely shocking! It went back 3 times, and still wasn't right.

Had a few issues with the exhaust showing signs of wear so decided to have a custom straight through built by the wizards at **Deutsch Tech** *and opted for quad carbon tips. At this time I was on the hunt for an air ride, but couldn't justify the £4.5-5k it would cost for a brand new set up. Fortunately I managed to find someone going from bags to coil overs, and snapped their arm off and purchased an Air Lift Performance V2 kit with 5 gallon tank & dual compressors.*

Spec list:

Roush limited edition
Custom straight through exhaust with quad carbon tips
Off road h pipe
Air Lift Performance V2 kit with 5 gallon tank & dual compressors
Trufiber A29 hood
Raxiom headlights
22" AC Forged 3 piece split rims
Spiked split rim bolts
True spike wheel nuts
True spike bullet antenna
LED side markers
Clear front indicators
Window tints
Roush under drive pulley
Steeda uprated rear discs
Custom dildo floor mats
Custom logo badges
Mapped

**I'm absolutely useless when it comes to cars so have professionals install all new parts.
Shout out To the following for looking after her:**

Paragon Auto – www.paragonauto.co.uk - WrapIt - @wrapitvehiclegraphics - Deutsch Tech - @deutschtech Custom Exotics - @custom_exotics1

Author: Paul Doherty

Helen Broomhall-Roberts
Subaru Impreza WRX JDM V7 Bugeye 2001

Instagram : @helenlouisewrx

I have been into cars for as long as I can remember, strange for a girl I know. As soon as I passed my test the first car I purchased was a Peugeot 106 1.6. It was my pride and joy and wasted no time starting on the mods. Think I spent about £4k just on a glitter paint job and body kit!

This was back in the Max Power days and Weston Wheels was the first proper show I attended and was proud to come 2nd in the Show n Shine. It was through the car scene that I met my now hubby who luckily for me was also mad about cars and has done most of the work on them too

After selling the Pug as I wanted to move on to bigger and better, I had a vast array of cars including various BMW's, Honda CRX del sol, three Toyota Supra's (I wish I hadn't sold them on!) on to an American left hand drive Ford Mustang and a highly modified Golf Gti on air bags. Most of these cars were all "show" cars and over the years I won trophies, cash and even a mountain bike for entering!

I then purchased a BMW Z4 which from years before I had always dreamt about owning. I finally got one and had it for about a year, putting on bigger wheels, body kit, straight through exhaust etc but there was always something missing and I couldn't figure out what it was.

Until one day back in May this year I was putting petrol in the Zed when I heard a rumbling and a Subaru Impreza pulled up next to me.

I looked across in absolute awe, it was stunning, and it was what I was missing.

This is my Subaru Impreza WRX JDM V7 Bugeye 2001.

After scouring the internet, I came across a recently imported Impreza, swapped it for the Zed and proudly drove home. It wasn't in the best state, didn't seem to be running right and needed a few bits repairing and replacing, but my hubby assured me it could be sorted. And how right was he.

When I got it home, we found the reason it wasn't pulling right was due to a dirty MAF, one squib of electrical cleaner and it was as smooth as silk. It was then a matter of sourcing some replacement OEM parts, trim bits etc.

The bonnet scoop was broken and had been stuck back together with carbon wrap, so I got a replacement courtesy of Pole Position UK. I got rid of the Japanese racing tyres as they were almost slicks and replaced them with some lovely Toyo Proxes Sports.

The whole car was cleaned, polished and waxed and came up like new. I was so pleased. We then moved on to the engine by putting on a Pipercross induction kit, Forge dump valve and a general tidy up and fresh graphics as the old ones were fading and peeling.

Although I had books and books of previous history paperwork, it was all in Japanese so it's difficult to know what has actually been done to it. At some point the back box had been replaced with a 3" stainless steel one but the centre pipe and resonators remained, so it was handed over to the guys at MIJ Exhaust in Walsall who replaced it with a straight through 3" stainless steel pipe and resonator delete.

Then the attention turned to the suspension which was quite a hard ride I have to say. After spending a few day's trying to source a locking bolt key for the spacers (a Japanese original) we managed to get the suspension off and replaced it with lovely Tein coil overs and a new set of discs and pads at the same time.

Once all that was done, we moved on to the interior and my talented hubby carbon wrapped the dash and fitted the Prosport gauges, new DVD head unit, upgraded the speakers and fitted a sub and amp in the boot.

Spec list at the moment is:

Tuning/Engine:

2.0 litre EJ20 4-cylinder Boxer, Sti tuned 16 valve, sequential gearbox
3" straight through stainless steel de-resonated exhaust system
Pipercross Induction Kit
Forge dump valve
Sti top mounted intercooler
Perrin pulley cover
Mishimoto oil cap
Chassis:

Tein Streetbasis Z adjustable coilovers Cusco strut brace
17" Oz Racing Superleggra gold alloys with Japanese spec spacers
Toyo Proxes Sport tyres
Rays lug nuts

Exterior:

Prodrive body kit, spoiler and bonnet scoop
Prodrive headlamps
Crystal tail lights, side indicators and repeaters
Lower front splitter
WRX rally mud flaps
Tinted windows
Subaru graphics

Interior:

Prosport centre console gauges
Digital lap timer and speedo
Carbon wrapped trim
JVC touch screen DVD head unit
JVC component speakers and tweeters Vibe Pulse 900 subwoofer powered by Kenwood amplifier

Picture's courtesy of @capturedbyneil

Thanks to Neil Broomhall-Roberts (@showoffs_inc) for all his hard work saving me probably £££ at a garage, we make a great team, my idea's and his talent!

Watch this space.

92 Honda Civic Hatchback
Sean

I'm 34 years old and I'm from The Dallas Oregon and for a living I'm a maintenance director at a senior home.

So here is a little about how I got into the car scene. I have always been into cars ever since I can remember all I ever wanted was hot wheels, rc cars, and monster trucks. As I got older I went from toys to import magazine's like super street and import tuner looking threw them finding what car I wanted when I got older and what I wanted to do to it.

So after a while I fell in love with the 92 Honda Civic hatchback and I started to make parts lists for everything I wanted to do to it from body mods to engine and interior everything. Started playing video games and all I ever wanted to do was modify cars in my video games like need for speed and mid night club.

Around that time which was 2001 the first fast and furious came out and I was hooked went to the movie theatre at least 12 times just to watch that movie and the car that stood out to me in the movie was Hector's 92 hatchback when he pulled up to (the racer's edge) in his gold hatchback at that point i said one day i will own one. I fell in love with that era.

The lights, body kits, outrageous sound system's, and all the customization on every ride, the cars themselves could tell you a story. It was awesome. When I was finally old enough to get my own car I got a 83 Cadillac Eldorado wasn't what I wanted but I was so happy I had my own car I could do something with whatever I wanted to do so I started small with it tinted the windows put a sound system in it but it just wasn't what I wanted so I ended up selling it and getting a truck.

Interior mods.
Diamond stitched armrest and cargo cover
in Jean material and yellow stitching,
Jean head liner,
Jean carpet,
Yellow painted plastics to match the paint outside, Blue and black carbon fibre bucket seat with
a blue harness bar and yellow braum harnesses, Blue quick release NRG steering wheel,

Going to fast forward to my first car I loved and that was a 89 Honda civic hatchback finally was able to start building a ride I was truly interesting in so I lowered it put wheels and tires on it, painted it, tinted the windows then I lost interest in it so few more cars went by and I finally ended up with a 92 civic hatchback that I ended up doing a boosted b18b1 motor swap in it.

Tein suspension, wheels and tires, del sol seats, and a sound system well that car was short lived got in a bad way had to sale it to pay bills.

After that I had a BMW I fixed up and then decided I needed to get back in the Honda game so I sold the BMW and picked up a 96 civic hatchback and that brings me to the car I own now.

It started off as a stock civic manual doors single cam y8 auto transmission so I started to modify it the way I wanted to. I started to realize that I stopped being interested in my other cars because I was doing it wrong by making them fast before I made them eye catching so I did it backwards this time.

So I started with the body mods first did an itr front end conversion wings west body kit modified as a widebody custom moulded from the front fenders all the way to the rear bumper then painted it yellow.

After that my kids were the ages of 3 and 7 and they said my car looked like a minion and so after that kind of ran with the theme. I converted my doors to power everything and then it took off from there to the mod list I have today which is.

Engine bay.

Swapped out the single cam and did a fully built b18b1 Bored out to 84mm with Darton sleeves,
CP piston's,
Manly rods,
Arp bolts,
Arp head studs,
Brian crower stage 2 turbo racing cams,
Brian crower springs and retainer's,
Ferrea valves,
Brian crower adjustable cam gears,
AEM fuel rail 1200cc injector's Edelbrock intake Manifold,
Skunk 2 throttle body,
HKS blow off valve,
Precision 6262 turbo,
Turbosmart wastegate,
Custom built 3in exhaust,
1000hp Insane shafts,
Sickspeed neo chrome lower control arms,
Sickspeed neo chrome solid motor mounts,
Sickspeed neo chrome fender bolts,
Radiator and oil cap, I did a 5 speed manual swap as well with hasport shift linkage and a sick speed short shifter, aem stand alone,

Author: Paul Doherty

Chris Shaw - Nissan 370z

Instagram: @getsh4wty_370z

I first got into cars about 1996 when I bought my first Max Power magazine in June 96 with the yellow Cossie with my school dinner money.

From then on my Dad would take me to shows like Donny and Max power live at NEC. I left school at 16 and started college as an apprentice mechanic and worked in 2 garage's learning. 4 years later I was a qualified mechanic and even did a 6 month's NVQ in valeting. In the end I gave this up as money wasn't great and am now in lower management, but I gained those invaluable skills during those years. First car was a replica Nova SRI to learn but at 18 my father let me buy the Ford Orion 1600 he'd bought at 2 year old when I was 10, so the car had huge sentimental value.

Sadly on 27th August 2003 this car was involved in an incident and was gone and I had my guardian angel out that day I think. Coincidentally that was the birthday of my Border collie , Topher I would adopt a few month's later. His name is now on my number plate. I did everything from bodywork, paint mechanic and ice and 5 years with this car I learnt a lot in the scene.

In the late 90s early 2000's my friends and I would be down Nott's circuit every single Sunday night parking up, watching street racing but obviously not doing it myself (wink) burnouts, going to cruises all over in convoy, all the good stuff that's dwindling today.

I've had so many cars from classic Impreza to SRT6 Crossfire's to Jaguar s type R. The decision to buy this 370z was one of luck and chance. I had saved up enough money to treat myself and at the time in 2016 I wanted a Ford Focus RS mk2 , but I didn't want to spend over 20k.

My second decision was a white 370z at 18k, but that car was over 100 mile's away, so I saw this yellow 370z just up the road and went to test drive it to get a feel and see if I like it. I fell in love with the car and this rare chicane yellow, which I later found out was 1 of 40 Nissan 370z Ultimate Edition's made.

Engine.

K&N in takes,
custom straight pipe with 5" tips

All metal work powder coated by @wheelfurb in Tamworth.

All plastics hydro dipped @tamworth_hydrodipping_services

Suspension.

Full airlift 3p kit with 4 gallon tank and twin Viair 444c Compressors both fitted with the addition of the very important check valve that do not come with the kit.

Interior.

Self built boot build for air ride with laminate floor.
Powder coated tank and all mounts by wheel refurb again.
Custom fabrication brackets and mounts made by @hollotmetalworks
Leather diamond floor mats and Alcantara trimmed various parts by myself.

Body.

Front lower Maxton designs front lip.
Genuine carbon fibre upper trim imported from the USA from The Z Store
Front upper Nismo moustache spoiler imported from USA. Evo-r bonnet vents.
Stillen canards
Custom polished aluminium billet front grill from USA.
Full custom head lights by myself, gloss back painted rear housing,
hydro dipped light shrouds,
custom clear glass hid lenses with 370z etched into lenses, Oracle twin halos with strobe function.
RGB demon eyes with blue tooth control.
Chameleon UV tint of front windscreen.
Full window tint in smoke.
Roof wrapped in colour changing Morpheus black by @tinttech_nottingham
A pillar and mirror wrapped in the same by myself.
Gloss black side steps.
Rear window louvres painted in Nissan's metallic black from USA
Rear lower diffuser in metallic black from Poland
Side rear window louvres by @vicrezcom again in metallic black from USA
Genuine carbon fibre rear spoiler by @crown_carbon_crafting imported from USA.

Photographer's

@tarjsnaps @jnovo19xx @pebe_automotive
@lasmalagzdinaphotography

Author: Paul Doherty

Warren Luff - MK4 Toyota Supra SZ

My name is Warren Luff, I'm a 20 year old Aeronautical Engineer from North Wales.

I first got into cars because of my father, he was a mechanic all his life and has worked on many iconic cars from the Escort, first gen Minis all the way over to the early Rx7s and everything in-between. I have been working on cars since I can remember and at 17, I decided to get my first car a mk3 Renault Clio. This made a good first car but was lacking in the power massively.

All my life I have been an adrenaline junky looking to push the limits. I then got myself a Yamaha r125 seeking speed. Due to my young age the bike also lacked in power, so I went back to my love of cars, this is when I bought my MK4 Toyota Supra SZ with a 2jz-ge engine at the age of 19.

This car is the dream of many people and was certainly one of mine and when the opportunity came in my life where I could waste all my money on a car, I took it to get my dream started. The car had a suspension problem and rocker cover leak but nothing I couldn't fix.

The previous owner had done the car up to look like the early GT40 with the baby blue paint, deep chrome rims and a super wide body kit. This was not to my liking, but I could see the potential in her, so I drove the car all the way back from Hull and started work on her. I fixed all the problems with the car by fitting all new gaskets throughout the engine all the way down to the head gasket. I also added Tein suspension in all 4 corners.

I hope one day to finally have the car looking and performing much better than a stock supra ever could.

The car has come a long way since then and has a long way to go. The car is very unique due to how wide it is and sitting on massive 335 wide rear tyres she stands out from the crowd.

If that wasn't enough the bright green paint and massive carbon wing should catch the eye of spectators at local meets of the groups I'm part of.

A Veilside body kit, with 3" rear wide arches and 1" wider fibreglass front arches.
Jap speed full carbon boot spoiler.
Veilside sun strip
A full respray in Kawasaki green form C.A.Re-finishing
SSR 3 decolt evolution 3 piece split rims. Sitting on 335/30/18 p zeros out back and 295/35/18 Michelin pilots out front
LS 400 4 pot floating callipers in green
EBC steel braided lines all round
Tein suspension
Cobra bucket seats
Sparaco 6 point harness
Sparaco 4 point harness
OMP deep dish wheel
Sparaco quick release
Completely striped out from rear seats back and painted black
centre strengthening harness bar
black carpets and roofing
2jz-ge engine
5 speed W58 gearbox
Carbon intake
Blue after market coolant hose
Electric blue rocker covers
Battery relocation to boot
Clear cam covers
Full engine rebuild to stock specks.

Some of the groups I'm in are Extreme BHP, Street Dreams, Modified North Wales and Supra Owners UK.

I hope one day to finally have the car looking and performing much better than a stock supra ever could. The car is being built to handle all situation's from drifting to racing yet still be drivable on the street as my supra is my daily car and I drive everywhere in it. The next thing coming up is a big single turbo build and hopefully pushing the 600BHP benchmark I have set so far.

This build will bc on my Instagram @WOZ1999 as the car develops in its life.

Author: Paul Doherty

Matt
2016 Ford Focus SE Hatchback

Instagram: @madfocus9

The compact Ford Focus is being discontinued in the U.S. It was originally set to be reimagined next year as a small crossover SUV-like wagon built in China called the Focus Active. However, Ford has since decided to cancel the wagon due to import tariffs that would make it unprofitable.

Hi all I'm Matt, I'm in the states in South Florida

A little about myself and my 2016 Ford Focus SE hatchback.

I have always been a Ford fan since I could remember playing with hot wheels as a kid. I'm a fan of all makes and builds, but Ford has my heart, even though they ripped my heart out by discontinuing the Focus line here in the States. That's a soap box for another time.

I came about my Focus after buying and selling 2 1975 F100s. I had a '75 Custom In-line6 short bed and flipped it after cleaning her up and getting the interior up to par. After that I bought my Kona Blue '75 F100 Ranger 302 all Edelbrock decked out with a short bed. After a couple years of owning her and wrenching every weekend, I had to sell her to a friend as she was taking up all my time from my 2 young boy's. Anyhow... onto the Focus.

I'll start out with the obvious, yes she is a SE trim, yet she's mine. I bought her in 2017 after I sold my truck and needed a daily that was good on gas. I've always been a fan of the MK3 look and when I saw her in the Ford Kona Blue, I drove over immediately and got rid of my Toyota Corolla and signed the papers.

I started off with the normal, tint and decals. Thinking about what I might want the Focus to look like. After thinking for a bit, and being a person that loves cars and seeing transformation of builds, I decided On what to do.

I decided on the colour scheme of gold and blue, a throw to my service in the United States Navy.

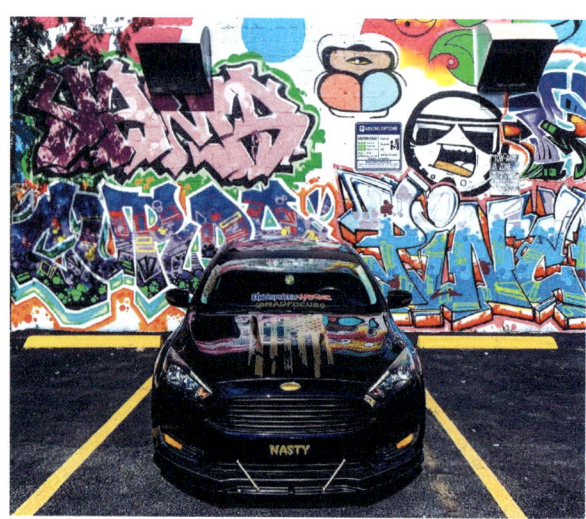

My first mod was the exhaust as I had missed the sound of the my '75 (so cherry) and bought the FSWERKS Race Exhaust. From there,

I began in October 2019 having some more fun.

I have a Custom Tune from Focus-Power (great custom tune). I swapped out the grill with the Titanium as I like the lines to all match the rest of the front end vs the honeycomb it came with.

Added the ST spoiler, Debadged and rearranged after painting them. Added the rear diffuser, rods and front lip/ splitter.

She needed some more love so I wrapped the reflector's and Ford emblem's in gold, and bought some gold lugs, mud flaps, lover's and painted the calliper's as well. I like to paint and do things myself. In December I bought Race land Coil overs and maxed it out for a 3 inch drop, (this I took to a buddies shop to do as I wanted to make sure she sat right) and dang she handle's so much better.

I needed some pop at night when I met up with the car crew that I have been family with since November of 2019, (Undisputed Vybez, IG: *@undisputedcrew* check us out). So I decided on the OPT7 under glow set and extensions for the grill. I love the glow and have always been a fan of them since I'm old school (age withheld).

I decided on the colour scheme of Gold and Blue, A throw to my service in the United States Navy. Hooyah!!

With the interior side of thing's, I swapped out the steering wheel with a 2017 Ford Escape, so I can have paddle shifters Vs. the electronic shift button on the shifter. Yes she's auto don't hate me, there wasn't a manual in Kona Blue at the lot. Anyhow, wrapped the wheel, painted the paddle shift extensions and installed her. Next on the list is deck out the interior a little with some paint or wrap, and get some custom flooring done.

I've mostly concentrated on the exterior of the Focus for now as I plan on getting a turbo kit from Focus-Power and didn't want it to waste money on things that were going to be replaced. Once the turbo kit is installed I'll be pretty set for a little bit before swapping out the transmission to a manual so I can go bigger turbo and play some more with mods.

Why don't I get an ST or RS some may ask? Well, I love my car and I'm having fun building her out the way I'd like her to be. I've got a family and knowing myself, I would get into too much trouble with more power.

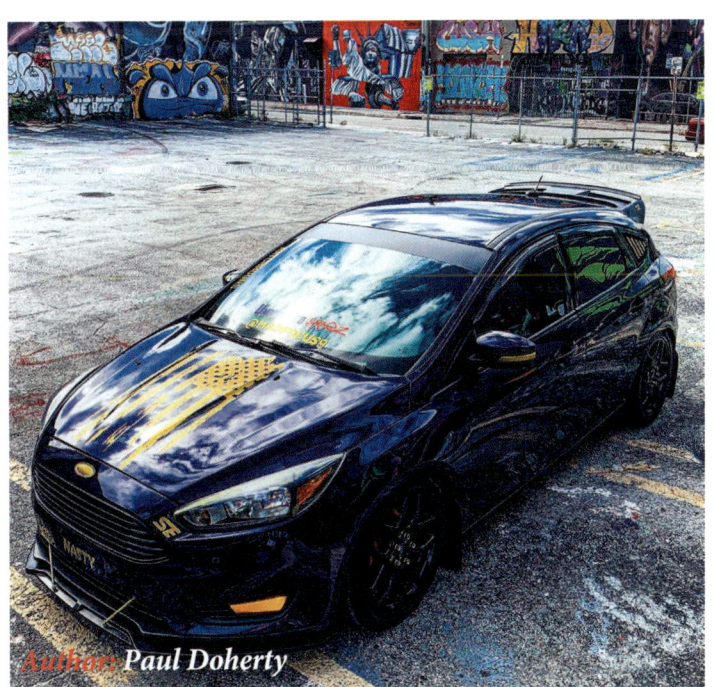

Author: Paul Doherty

Mikey Rowlands
Mk2 Ford Focus RSEdition

Instagram: @Trigaz_sti
YouTube - MikeyRowlandsRS

Hey I'm Mikey Rowlands, I'm 26 from north Wales
I was brought up with rally cars from a very early age as my father was a rally driver, having his and many of his friends rally cars built on our driveway (mainly Mk2 Escorts), my father built his wide arched RWD converted Cosworth powered Ford Fiesta Mk3 XR2 in his garage, Growing up around all those rally cars you can see that's where my love for Fords came from.

The first time I ever wanted a Focus RS was when I saw Mikko Hirvonen testing his Focus WRC on the Cambrian rally back in 2009, after seeing it going sideways around a corner at like 80mph I instantly fell in love and knew I needed to own a Focus ha-ha!

Jump forward a few years and I came across Rich Fox's WRC inspired Mk2 FOCUS RS on Jamie_FYD's YouTube channel and it instantly reignited my love for them and I knew that I needed to own one.

In 2018 I finally got my hands on my Mk2 Focus RS after dreaming of owning one!

The car was completely stock when I first bought it and my original plan was to keep it stock… yeah.. so… after talking to a few ST/RS owner's about mods I could do to make it sound / perform better.. Before I knew it I had dropped some serious ££££ and then I had a strong custom stage 2 400bhp / 600nmt RS with crackles, big flame's & anti-lag tuned by DDG in Manchester @ddgremapping.

Full spec -

Previously - Revo Stage 2 'BD Performance Wrexham'
Currently - Custom Stage 2 'DDG Remapping Manchester'

AirTec Stage 3 Intercooler
AirTec 3.5" Downpipe
AirTec Plenum
Airtec Big boost pipes
Pro Hoses Full upgrade
Group A K&N induction kit
Turbosmart Recirc valve
Turbosmart Actuator
Milltek Exhaust system
Eibach 30mm Lowering Springs
Rear Eibach 25mm Spacers
Front Eibach 20mm Spacers
ACR WRC Bonnet Vents
KMS WRC Roof Scoop
Carbon Fibre Style Engine Covers Autobeam
Strobe Wing Mirror Indicators Autobean Full light upgrade
Maxton Design full Splitter kit
Kode Steering wheel
B-G Quick relea
Custom Led Rear Tail lights
Custom Headlights
Custom Halo Fog Lights
Rallyflapz Mud Flaps
Autowatch Ghost

Author: Paul Doherty

Driving my RS always puts a smile on my face and it always turns peoples heads (sometimes for the wrong reasons haha) but I can honestly say I've never had a dull moment owning it!

Yes it can go wrong and cost me a lot of money but just seeing it sitting on my driveway or parked up somewhere and thinking to myself, "that's my car! I own that!" There's no better feeling!

Since owning the car I've met some pretty cool people and have had some amazing experience's, i always find it amazing how a car can bring so many like minded individuals together!

The amount of message's / comments I get on my Instagram from people telling me how much they like my car truly means a lot and for once in my life It seems like I must be doing something right haha!

I'm so grateful that I'm lucky enough to have the chance to own what I think will go down as a historical part of Ford history that is the Mk2 Ford Focus RS!

The car is nowhere near finished yet as I have some pretty big plans for it coming up in 2021, just to list a few In the next few month's it'll be going in for a fully Forged engine rebuild by @BDPerformance in Wrexham.

I've had a great ongoing relationship with Darren and the lad's at **BD Performance** and highly recommend them!

I'm also going down the WRC route and will be getting a M-Sport WRC Spoiler, **AUTO SPECIALISTS** Front and Rear WRC Bumpers and to finish it all off nicely a M-Sport inspired rally livery!

Instagram: @SONICST_180

Jake Hopkins
Fiesta mk7 ST - SONIC ST

Hi all I'm Jake Hopkins I live in Coventry West Midlands

I am currently doing my level 3 apprenticeship in Mechanic's and have always been into Fords from a very young age from collecting Fast-ford magazine's

SONICST was my daily for the first year I owned him, then it's just used for show season.

The journey with Sonic started in 2017 when I brought him brand new with 5 mile's on the clock it is now at 26k in 3 years, It's currently running stage 2 pro with decel from AET MOTORSPORT and the long term plans are to eventually build the engine and go stage 4, at some point go full Airtec wide arch, Airtec wing, Bola b10 wheels, BC racing coilovers, Airtec show cage.

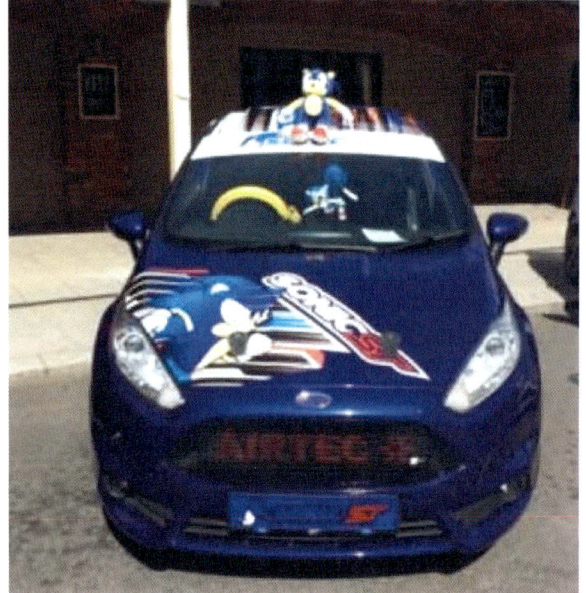

The mk7 ST, For me, the spirit blue has to be one of the best colours.

It has been the best 3 years, I have met so many great people in the car scene and enjoyed going to shows and meets showing SONICST of, a lot of people in the Ford scene now know me and SONICST, which is cool.

The best part of being in the car scene is getting up early in the morning and driving to a show.

SONICST is a unique design wrap done by @blueprint_nottingham. I gave them an idea I had in my head and they smashed the wrap out of the park. I've always loved being different and you can see you won't see another sonic wrapped Fiesta ST. Every time SONICST does go out he's always getting spotted because he is unique.

With Fiesta ST's there is so much you can do modification wise and that's why I love them.

Performance

ITG full induction all the way to the turbo
Stage 3 Airtec intercooler
3 Inch VUDU downpipe VUDU short shifter Mountune cat back
Michelin ps4 tyre's
VUDU front discs
Ferodo ds2500 pads

Exterior

SONICST wrap
Auto beam LED lights

I have always done shows with @FordMania the owner Ian Taylor and his son James Taylor have always made me feel welcome from my first ever show in August 2017 Ford Fair and now am an Admin for the club which I am very Proud of.

Author: Paul Doherty

Ryan Blythe — Audi A3 8v PFL

Instagram @stealth_a3_8v

I'm Ryan Blythe, I'm 22. I live in Peterborough, England. I drive an Audi A3 S-line.

I work full time away from home so I daily the car and do a lot of mile's in it. I do all my own work and maintenance that needs doing.

I've always been interested in Motorsport and the car scene, from a young age I would watch top gear over and over, had one of them toy car matt's and a big selection of hot wheels. I was fortunate to get to help out and work in the pits/Hospitality for Power Maxed Racing in the BTCC.

I bought the car from a dealer, kept it standard for about a month before I started putting my own spin on things. After a while I had my own unique style on it and over time I went through different colours and style's.

About a year in I set on going for the Murdered out look, the all black.

Why this car? For me I had a long look around test drive loads before I came across the Audi straight away. I fell in love with it, ever since I've just had a passion for Audi's.

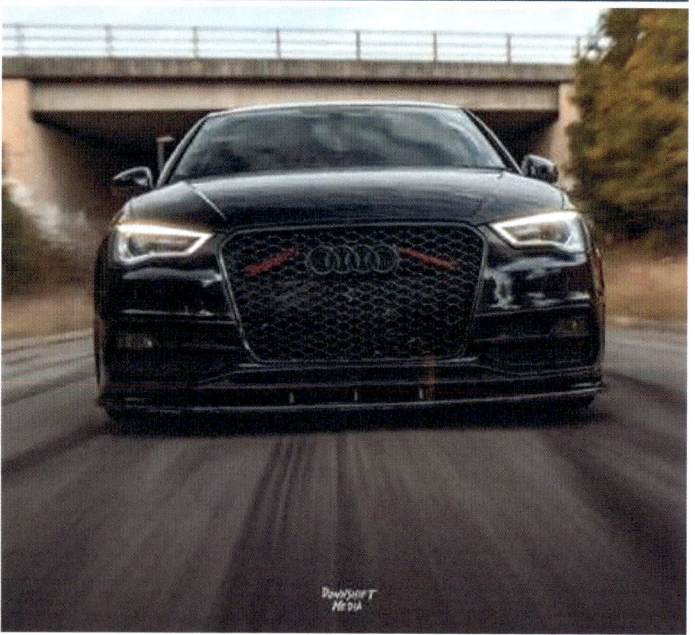

I wouldn't say mine is unique compared to others but I will say it's unique to me.

I've built it for how I want it. Got big things coming in the future to take it to the next level.

This is my Audi A3 8v PFL

It's a 1.4 tfsi S-line

Spec list;

Stage 1 map
Lowers on coilovers
Rs honey Comb grill
TRC splitter
Maxton design side skirts, rear diffuser extension and spoiler extension
De-chrome all round
De-badge
Rear light tints
De-wiper
Inside red trims and vent rings
Rotifrom KPS 8.5j 18s wheels wrapped in Continental contact sports 215/40/18
Polybush suspension
Stock brakes upgrade to Brembo pads and grooved disk's Pace car indicators
Custom stainless steel exhaust decat Downpipe to quad tips

Photographer's:
@down.shift.media
@untypical_media

The car scene definitely takes up a lot of time and commitment, I'm always trying new stuff and working on the car.

With my car being black I'm always cleaning and polishing to keep high standards.

I'm grateful for the fact that my girlfriend is interested in the car scene and supports me all the time even if I'm cancelling on her to go to a show or a shot.

I've met some awesome friends because of the car scene and been to some amazing shows including

Tucked automotive meet and eat pt1/2, Rollhard show and broke boy's show's.

It's a shame as this year would have been the first indoor show at the ultimate show in Liverpool, fingers crossed for next year.

I was in the scene a little by going to meets and doing the club side of things at first but I wouldn't say I was in the scene properly till I met Rob from @down.shift.media doing a shot on my car, his work is outstanding and just gives everything produced high standards. He's helped me a lot with meeting new

people and giving me opportunities to showcase the car at events along with other top quality motors.

Groups and clubs - I'm in a lot of clubs but for me the ones that stand out are:

Car collective (@car_collective) because for them it's not about what you drive, it's about the drive and being one big family. they put on amazing drives and events.
Tucked automotive (@tucked_) I have always followed their progress as an automotive brand, their rage is just top quality and is always above expectation's. They are very welcoming and have put on some, if not the best events I've been to.
Vag society (@vagsocietyuk) for me this club fits very well, I love the whole vibe that they set at there meets and the love they show to all builds.

Author: Paul Doherty

Lauren Talbot
Mk1 Eunos

I'm Lauren Talbot, this is my Mk1 Eunos

I live in a small village in the Norfolk countryside. I own a Dog Grooming salon, which funds my cars and my drifting hobby.

Since I can remember I have always been into cars. Growing up I was always one for racing games on the Playstation1. My oldest brother and his friends when I was growing up were always messing around with their cars, mostly Fords, which is where my love for classic Fords comes from.

When I was 15 one of our friends tragically lost his life in his Fiesta mk3 RS Turbo, and I think that when I really got into cars, seeing the modified car community all coming together to celebrate his life, so I set out to build a car I knew would make him proud

I have had a fair few cars in my 11 years of driving, my very first car was a Ford KA which was bought for me after I passed my driving test, and that was when my true love to modify cars started. from that I moved on to my Ford Escort XR3i which I bought back in 2012, which I still have and is currently undergoing a full restoration. A few other cars I have owned are a Nissan 200sx s13, Toyota Paseo, BMW e46 328ci Mazda RX8 and of course my mk1 Eunos Roadster.

Most of my cars are modified one way or another, but my most highly modified car is my mk1 Eunos.

I bought my Eunos back in April 2015, it was an accidental purchase off Ebay, never thinking the seller would accept my low offer on the car. Then a 400 mile round trip to collect the car. When I purchased the car she was in a pretty sorry state, the red paint was faded and lacquer peeling everywhere, and it started but didn't drive. After a new slave cylinder and about 3 hour's of bleeding the clutch, I was finally able to get the car into gear and for the first time drive her! I remember that day like it was yesterday, driving it around the private industrial park absolutely overjoyed, with the biggest smile on my face, I didn't want to stop driving her. My next task was to sort the paint out on the car. I had previously purchased some magenta pink car paint for a previous car which I never used, so I decided that rather than trying to revive the red paint, I would just paint my Eunos pink, thus Martha Pink Miata was born!

I had purchased my show tickets for Modified Nationals that year with my old car club 'Car Chick Society' which then set the deadline to get the car ready by, which only gave us 2 weeks to get everything done. We called a friend who was a sprayer to come in and help get the car show ready, we done it all in one day, working all day and part way through the night to get the bodywork finished on the Friday ready for the show on Sunday, we pulled it off and Martha went to her very first show in 2015..

When I bought the car it was never intended for her to turn into a show car, she was meant to be a drift car, which for a short time she was, I took her on a track drift day at my local track 'Norfolk Arena' which is now the Adrian Flux Arena. But then one thing led to another and before I knew it she was a show worthy car which I no longer wanted to risk on the track, so I bought myself a purpose built BMW e36 as a new drift car.

Shortly after buying the car I found a hard top roof for sale in black locally, which I snapped up, as the soft top wasn't in the best of conditions. And from there I did a few small modifications like wheels and interior bits, such as a rear 5race 4 point roll bar, driver's bucket seat and harness, NRG steering wheel set up snap off boss and Nardi steering wheel.

Then in 2016 for my birthday I received my bodykit for the car, an Arios rear bumper, Bomex side skirts and a Zenda front bumper, all imported from Japan, so it was decided that the whole car was going to get another full respray so the kit matched, but this time I decided to add a little bit (a lot) of glitter in to it as well. I then did some suspension upgrade to coilovers and a new exhaust system with removable Bozo pipes, which got me into a little bit of trouble with the police, so I sadly had to remove them.

Then in July 2016 my engine sadly died after the woodruff key was damaged when the cam-belt was changed. Luckily I had purchased a second Eunos a couple months earlier with the same engine with very low mile's, so me and a couple friends spent the weekend changing the engine over, which in the process I removed the aircon system and changed the power steering rack, for a depowered steering rack, as I love the feeling of driving a car without PAS. After the engine swap and a couple niggly problem's along the way with injector's and fuel rail, Martha lived again!

I decided that I wanted to go wider with my Eunos, so I purchased some new alloys, Rota Grid V, the front wheels are 15x8 et0 and the rears are 15x9 et0. I took my car to a friend of mine Rich who owns a bodyshop called DV8 and he rolled my arches out for me so I could fit my new wheels. In April 2017 I then decided to purchase some new coilovers from Driftworks, HSD's.

While at a show that year I spoke to SuperPro about a full polybush set up for the car, I was given a card and asked to contact them about a potential sponsorship. But sadly before I was emailed them, the worst thing imaginable happened. While parked up at a meet, a driver lost control of his car a solid straight into the passenger side of my car causing over 3000 pounds worth of damage.

My heart just sunk, I was in shock and total disbelief about what had just happened, a car that I have spent the last 2 and a half years building, was a potential write off in a split second. When Brentacre, my car insurance heard what had happened, they made it their mission to get Martha sorted and make sure the car wasn't a write off. Which is where we have respray number 3.

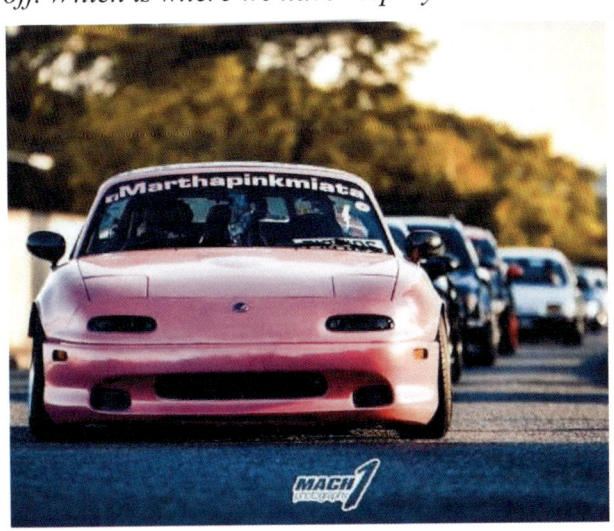

Once everything with the insurance was settled, I booked the car in to be repaired and resprayed, however this time I was going to be adding some big changes to the car's appearance while it was in the spray shop. I had a vision in my head to make my Eunos stand out even more and become even more unique.

I decided that I wanted it to be even wider, so I had the rear arches flared out even more and I had the original front wings made wider, and decided that I wanted to go with a smooth finish on the car, so I had the all lines in the car and rear bumper smoothed.

I got the car back in front of the body shop in November. Start of 2018 I borrowed my friends workshop with a set of ramps, and me and a couple of friends totally stripped the underside of the car, we moved the subframes and all the arms, and I sent everything away to be sandblasted.

When I got everything back I painted it all gold and fitted my new polybush kit and adjustable ARB's, as well as upgrading my clutch and brakes.

The car was resprayed yet again, and again I decided on something a little different, still remained with the pink theme, however this time I decided to go with full Spectraflare on the car, the only car in the country to be fully Spectraflare.

The mod list for the Euro's so far

Arios rear bumper
Bomex side skirts
Zender front bumper
Customer wide front wings
Flared wide arches front and rear
Smoothed bodywork
Custom paint
Rota Grid-V alloys 15x8 et0 front 15x9 et0 rear
full SuperPro poly bush kit
SuperPro front and rear adjustable ARB's Jasma imported manifold/downpipe Powerflow Stainless exhaust and backbox HSD coilovers Tinted TSI's
Chameleon halo headlights
Ducktail spoiler
Hard top roof
5Race 4 point roll bar
Corbeau driver seat
Pink Luke harness
Nardi half dish steering wheel
NRG slim boss
NRG slim quick release
Jimmy Up gear shifter
Custom door cards

The car has been to many many shows, securing indoor slots at gravity 2 years in a row. Most of the shows I go to, I attend with my club Fuelled Collective, and shows not with my club I always enter it into show and shine. The car is still far from finished 5 years on, with another complete custom respray in the pipeline to fix a couple of issue's I have been having with the current paint on the car. The interior is going to have a complete makeover, with custom door cars already fitted. I have another sponsorship waiting with Corbeau which has already been agreed.

I am proud to say that most of the work on the car has been carried out by myself with help from friends along the way. When I decided I was going to build a show car, I wanted to do it myself, rather than someone else doing it all for me. It's taken a long time so far, but it has been worth the time spent, the countless days, untold amounts of money, stress and bloodied knuckles, it has all been worth it.

To get into my car and drive it, the feeling I get, smiling from ear to ear, and seeing the reaction I get from other people, nothing can quite compare to that.

I didn't build the car to be the best modified car, I don't really enter the competitions at shows, I built it for the love of the car and the modified car scene.

My dream car, aside from my Eunos, would have to be a full Rocket Bunny Nissan s13. One of my biggest regrets was selling my first s13.

Author: Andz Stinton

Instagram: @the_mistress_vrs

Tom
Mk1 Octavia vrs

Hey I'm Tom

I'm 29 years old and I'm from Stoke on Trent born and bred.

I'm a construction hoist installer but an electrician by trade so I'm definitely not afraid to get my hands dirty. I'm proud to say my car is definitely built, not bought!

If I'm not at work you will most probably find me under the bonnet of my car!

Cars have been my passion for as long as I can remember. Working on cars with my Dad and Grandad from a very young age it was a given that it would continue into my adult life. My first car was a 1995 reg corsa b 1.2 8 valve in red which I modified with my dad Max power style.

I then went on to own another 2 of these a silver 2000 reg 1.2 16 valve and a black 2000 reg 1.6 16 valve sport with a custom built inlet and throttle body taking standard 106 break power to a mighty 116.3 Bhp, it was a little pocket rocket and so much fun to drive even if I did flood the engine within a week when I misjudged the depth of a puddle.

I owned a 2002 reg silver Volvo s60 2.4 D5 early life crisis car (in mourning for the death of my black beauty) and then bought a 2008 reg vectra c 1.9ctdi which again was modified with full Irmscher kit stage 2 map pushing 197 Bhp 445nm torque.

Completing the look with 100 edition alloys bonnet reflector and tiger stripe vinyl decals, but as a diesel I missed that noise of the loud exhaust. I bought the Skoda in 2019 after the downfall of the vectra
(water pump failed) and instantly fell back in love! Petrol passion.

Since owning the car I have spent my time creating something that is unique and mine! Becoming heavily involved in the car scene attending local and not so local meets. The car scene in stoke is starting to build back up to the former glory days of festival parks with Clubs United that meet as often as they can with up to 1000 cars.

We have started to attend a lot of car shows including Tunerfest, Trax, regional meets, Himley hall classic and retro show, forge action day, action finale at Castle Combe and more!

There is no better feeling than driving in a convoy with many other modified cars to a meet and I love the buzz and adrenaline it brings. It's amazing to meet fellow car enthusiasts and really nice when someone admires the car.

We recently had a rep from a car club who was desperate to see this car in person and travelled from Birmingham to stoke for a meet and happened to stumble across it. Needless to say he was very impressed with the car and I was very proud to receive some of the comments I was given.

A little back story on the name is the wife... she decided to call it the mistress and said it is because of the amount of time and money it takes up in my life but she love's it just as much as I do if not more!

When I'm having a bad day with it and I feel like stripping and selling the parts she always talks me out of it as she definitely has developed a soft spot for her.

The rally red paintwork on the car was very undesirable and had a lot of bad lacquer peel and a really bad driver side rear door repair and respray, but it gave me something to work with.

I looked at having the car resprayed but wanted something different to the ordinary red so I decided to have a custom wrap and livery put on it to hide a lot of damage and bad paint.

The wrap itself is crazy in the way the colours change as the light hits it. It can look candy red to orange and even a tinge of purple in darker lighting Interior- mk4 golf anniversary Recaro leather seats with tall headrests.

In the engine bay I am going for the minimal look because I love an empty tidy bay. Also it makes working on the engine easier as there is more room to get to those hard to reach places. It's always nice to see your hard work pays off.

I do all the work on my car myself and never owning a petrol turbo powered engine I started with minimal knowledge on how they work. Getting stuck in and hands on with it has allowed me to get to know these engines inside and out!

I've had a lot of knowledge and advice from people on the mk1 page's on Facebook and the Vag groups but getting my hands dirty and taking things apart myself is the best way I learn.

Since the article was released we have gone for full custom livery up the side's that mirror each other. I have completed a full engine change over 1 weekend and have had custom powder coated inlet, camshaft cover and heat plate in metallic fleck candy red.

A full custom stage 2 map with no lift shift, over run and launch control. Still to have it dynoed but will be expecting around the 250-60 Bhp mark with the results.

A lot of hard work and effort put into it over a short amount of time! Very pleased with the results and feel very lucky to be able to share my car with stance auto reader's.

I wasn't happy with the paintwork that was still on show as the roof had faded to pink (the worst problem with red cars) so this was removed after only 3 months and me and my wife decided to wrap the car ourselves at home over a few weeks and luckily very nice weather that was on our side!

Fully stripped and ready to wrap! Being complete novice's at wrapping, we began and with a lot of hard work and some amazing advice from a friend who works for wrap extreme we managed to complete the job!

We have since added decals in white to make the wrap stand out a little more.

We added the black triangle's on the back to break the red up and to make it stand out because I like to be different.

Engine -

evap pipe deletes,
painted rocker cover,
Painted inlet manifold,
throttle body and intercooler pipes in matt red.
Engine mounts painted black.
Top custom intercooler pipe wrapped in red heat wrap. Chrome strut brace.
Large black welly style intercooler from creation's Motorsport with custom pipework and custom writing. Gearbox linkage updated bushes.
Phenolic inlet manifold spacer.
Clocked throttle body.
Large ramair induction kit with cold air induction pipe (behind front bumper).
Coil Pack stainless cover from ADP auto works
Custom inlet trim cover currently being mocked up.
Custom made under bonnet mirror plate's. Straight through exhaust with a large oval tip. Show style red horns.
Hard-line deletes.
Sai, n249, carbon canister deletes.
Pas reservoir and screen wash relocated. Under Bonnet lights.
Coolant bottle delete.
Battery relocation and full wire tuck.
Stage 2 map with anti lag, launch control, no lift shift and overrun.
Told the map pulls at 240 Bhp but is looking to get back on the dyno as soon as possible.

The car has probably spent more time on axle stands than on the road.

I had a few troubles chasing a bad boost leak and then a faulty turbo which when changed failed again so in went another turbo which I managed to change in 2 hours!

Also had bad splitter damage when the bumper dropped on the way home from a meet in derby but this has been fixed and re attached.

I don't do subtle and love having a car that stands out of the crowd.

Next on the list of never ending jobs is:

re-routing the turbo to front block pipe and braided fuel line routed around the right of the engine to tidy up the left hand side.

Remove all spare brackets.
Custom gear gaiter/knob/handbrake.
Potentially custom seats, door cards and dash.

It's definitely a car that puts a smile on my face and there is more to come! The following of these cars is amazing and I can honestly say I have made so many lifelong friends through the Skoda car scene!

The entire list of all my Mods can be found on my Online Feature at :-

WWW.STANCEAUTO.CO.UK.

Spec List

Kolor Koncept red seat belts.
Genuine l and k leather door cards.
Vrs puddle lights.
Audi TT knee bars.
Audi s3 steering wheel with Skoda emblems. Golf mk4 black carpet.
Drivers side gauge pod with boost gauge. Custom a pillar 3 gauge pod with voltage, oil pressure and oil temperature.
Pioneer double din stereo system.
Upgraded speakers throughout.
Custom headlining lights in red and boot neon's.
Custom boot build in progress consisting of custom built red and black leather surrounds with 12" in phase subwoofer and in phase amp on show. 2 small pioneer black and red speakers. Looking at adding another 2 matching subs either side of the boot to finish the look off.
Led lights all around.
Newer style embroidered Vrs black and red floor mats. Rare sunglasses holder in place of Drivers side grab handle. **Continued Online:--**

Author: Andz Stinton

Laura Marie
Bagged mk3 scirocco

Instagram: @laura_mariexo

Hi I'm Laura Marie, This is my Bagged mk3 Scirocco

Well my life in the car scene hasn't been very big at the beginning, last year I was able to go to my first shows @rollhard, @ultimatestanceshow, @lowdown and @edition38 where I met such friendly people and went there with good mate's.

Just before @lowdown I decided to purchase another car to be able to go to shows, that was where I was able to pick up a black Scirocco. I was so happy with it.. yes it needed work but it was such a good project and a car I always wanted.

After a few weeks of owning, it was already on a new set of wheels, my first set of @3sdms and also lowered. I loved the look but still wasn't happy. I was then able to pick up air suspension a few months later and it was the best buy, plus a new set of @3sdms 19 inch.

Spec list

Front bumper pre Facelift
Back r bumper
Side skirts
Cup spoiler
Rotiforms
Custom headlights
Eyebrows
Ramair filter
Full colour respray
Fully debadged
Full custom exhaust
Splitter and side skirt extensions Carbon plastic interior Bootbuild
Air suspension

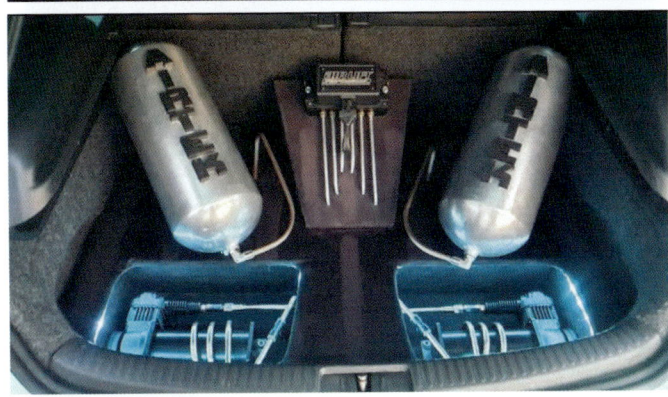

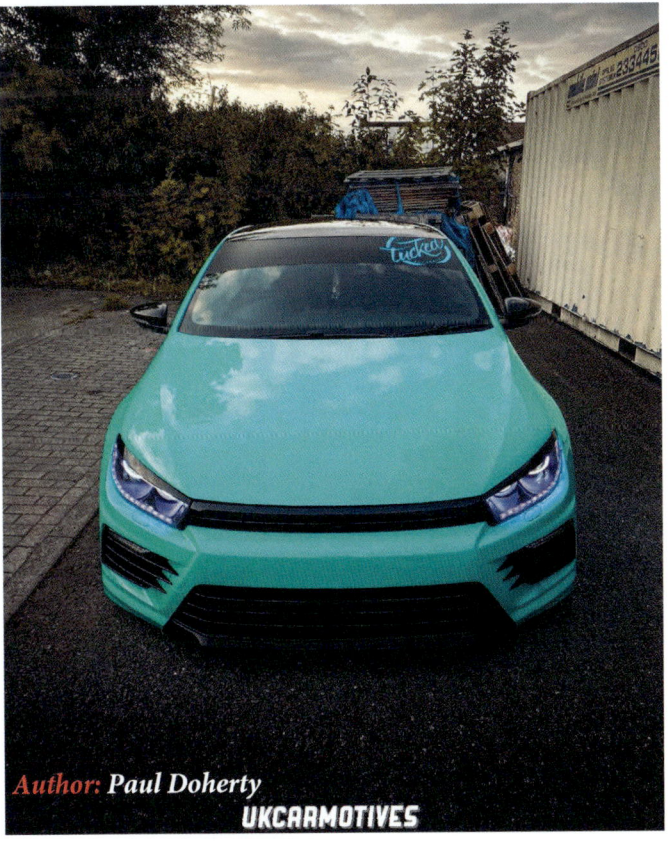

Author: Paul Doherty

I was so happy with it, until I realised I wanted to build it more and make it a show car. I upgraded the front and back bumpers, added a cup spoiler and side skirts. Then I took it to have a wrap done where it went satin black holographic.

Again I loved the wrap but the quality wasn't all there... At that time as well I was able to get my boot built by @airtek_automotive. Also a full custom exhaust from @sportssystem it was coming along so well.

I was able to attend @ultimate_dubs_uk where I got into the show and shine outside. I was unbelievably happy, but I wanted to do better.

The last show I attended with the satin car @tucked meet and eat, where I also met some new people , but was also looking forward to seeing my car stand out from the rest after it was finished.

A few weeks ago I was in the body shop @zprayprocustomization where after months of choosing a colour and not seeing it for a few weeks. Plus another set of wheels, this time @rotiforms i was finally able to see it and the new look.

Plus the new custom headlights and the extension from @maxtondesign I was finally happy with the final product.

The final show of attending this year @tucked meet and eat part 2. Where I was finally able to show the car off, I had so much attention because of the colour and the way it sat, I was sent so many pictures and had a lot of conversation's and positive comments about the car.

I definitely enjoy the car scene. The people I have met and talked to over the years have inspired me to build the car how I want. Meeting people and just generally having a really good time.

I have also met some amazing photographer's @ukcarmotives, @Down.shift.media and @mk_automotive_ who have been there since I first got the Scirocco and new photographer's @jakewardphoto, @lowdown @tucked

I have a local network of friends interested in the car scene but not directly tied to a group or club, but making new friends each show and meets that I attend.
At the moment it's a finished product, but I'm also up for a change. Next might possibly be interior. If I was able to find seats I want then that will be my next purchase and upgrade. But will also have custom seat skins made for the seats.
A big shout out to my car detailer as well who does a fantastic job @glodekprestigedetailing

All I can say is a big thank you to all the people who were involved in the build, the support and companies who have helped me get the car ready and the way that I want. Plus the photographer's who have been there to take these amazing pictures.

Nissan Skyline R34 GTT
Lee Adler
Instagram: @lee_adler

My name is Lee, I'm a European business functional analyst for a welding firm.

Since I was a young boy I've always been into cars; going to car shows with my then step dad, cruises to Southend when it was less about modern cars and more about classics and subscription's to all the car magazine's of the day.

I remember having pictures on the wall of cars like the Bugatti EB-110 and the Ferrari F40, cars I still dream about owning today, but what really sealed the deal was fast forwarding to 1999 when I was 16, and getting a copy of Gran Turismo 2. One of the cars that made it's debut on it just captivated me and commanded attention and saw HOURS of play time; the Nissan Skyline R34 GTT and since then it was always my dream car.

My first car when I was 17 was far removed from the R34 though, it was a Peugeot 205 automatic, followed quickly by a Nova 1.3sr which was the first car I modified.

But after falling in love with the Skyline, I had Japanese car blood running through my veins so as soon as budget allowed I moved into the world of Jap cars - as did my friends.

I've had a lot of Skyline's over the years, never really going to town modifying them as they weren't 'the one' but an opportunity arose to get a very nice and pretty much standard R34 GTT.

Don't let the lack of a GTR badge fool you - these are still very capable cars with the strong neo engine but with two major benefits over the GTR platform; RWD and also they are the underdog.

The fact that people always say 'oh it's only a GTT' has helped guide my modification process. The exterior I have kept relatively stock looking - with subtle styling upgrades, the interior is OEM+ with most interior plastics replaced, cleaned, retrimmed or customised - but the monster that lurks under the bonnet is what separates it from the crowd and makes people pay attention; a massively high spec RIPS RB30 - sourced and built by Richard Bell (Bells Auto Service's).

Is the project finished? No not even close. I still have plans to do something tricky with the gearbox, full respray and more re-trimming and custom seats... amongst other things.

The car is part of me now, I can't see me ever parting with it. It's everything I ever wanted from a modified car and more and puts a MASSIVE smile on my face whenever I drive it.

The current Spec list is as follows:

Power: 640bhp Torque: 530ft/lb

You can always catch me on the Skyline Owners Forum or at local meets every now and then. Looking forward to Yakushi coming up in September too which is always a pleasure to attend.

Massive thanks to:

Richard Bell @BellsAutoServices for building a beast of an engine and the tuning,

Wayne Taylor @AutoExtreme_ltd, Paul Howard @JDMGarageuk

The team at Garage D for supplying parts and doing the odd job here and there for me too.

Engine

RIPS RB30 block and crank.
Cylinders bored to 86.5mm & refaced RIPS Steel con rods
RIPS Extended baffled sump
CP Forged pistons and rings
Extended crank nose
N1 oil pump
ARP Head studs

Just A taster of the Mods, it is far to large to Print it all, if you would like to see my entire list and what I pretty much spent all my money on head over to:-

www.stanceauto.co.uk

Here you will find my Online Magazine Feature along with Hundreds of other Hi-class cars

Instagram: @b6_ocd

Adam Waggott
Audi 1.8 T B6

I'm from Bournemouth Dorset and I'm a logistics manager for a toy wholesale company based in Bournemouth.

The car I own is an Audi A4 1.8t and is a very well-known car in the show community and is sponsored by juicy details a very well known car product and detailing brand in the UK.

I got into the car scene about 10 years ago I just loved the whole social side of meets and shows and looking at other people's builds which would help me push my limits on building cars I started with just Vauxhall nova's and putting the 2.0l red top in them as they are such fun cars to drive.

Then I progressed to Jap cars such as Subaru's and Nissan 200sx as they are just raw cars to drive and are so easy to work on.

My current car which is an Audi 1.8t B6 is very well known as it's now on it's second look as it used to have bride low Max seats with Tanaka harnesses the car was built with an Japanese inspired look which upset a lot of purist's but it's not about what everyone else is doing you need to follow your own idea's in this scene as that's what gets you noticed and gained me magazine feature's.

After that happened in winter last year I felt it was time to take the car totally apart and start all over again to make it look totally different and this is definitely the best look it's had and will probably be the last as this time the car almost broke me.

Especially when trying to fit the huge Porsche brakes it boasts all round and trying to get the wilwood handbrake calliper to work with the self-adjusting lever was a total nightmare but we got there in the end.

It's one of the pleasure's I get from building the car myself as you everything that's been done to it and makes you extremely knowledgeable about the car as a lot people will say you can't make that fit and it's a case of I will make it fit.

When it's show season the shows that we normally attend are players as it's such a great atmosphere. @Fitteduk, @Worthersee, @ultimate dubs, Gravity, @Edition38 there are also a few more we do as well.

It's not about what everyone else is doing you need to follow your own ideas.

Interior

Recaro wingbacks with custom red carbon backs seats are retrimmed in red leather with cross stitching. Flocked brown dash and door cards with matching leather trim. Red Carbon pillar covers all trim in red carbon. Arm rest in red carbon. Rear mirror in red carbon. RS4 flat bottom steering with trimmed in red leather and red carbon. Flocked glove box and lower dash. Flocked black centre console. Black RS4 headlining and pillars. Show cage fitted and painted in Acid green.

Tuning

Audi A4 1.8t 20v freshly rebuilt this year by myself and Josh at @josh_ iconautomotive K03sTurbo,decat pipe, straight pipe exhaust system, ram air induction. Mapped by @ozmomotorsport. Carbon engine Cover, Carbon Scuttle Panel, Carbon ecu cover, Carbon battery cover, Carbon Bonnet strut

Chassis

19x9.5 Ispiri FFP1 (rear) 19x8.5 Ispiri FFP1 (front) in carbon graphite with 235 35 19 tyre's all round. Airrex Air suspension including Airrex Struts. Porsche Calipers Z18 up front with 380mm discs and Porsche rear calipers with wilwood handbrake calipers painted in acid green.

Styling

Paint Misano red with black roof by PMC Bodywork's. Factory spec votex model with smoothed front bumper, JE designs window spoiler.. Depo front and rear lights .B7 RS4 wing mirrors with red carbon base plate's. Red carbon pillars. Maxtron RS4 front splitter. Heko front wind deflector's

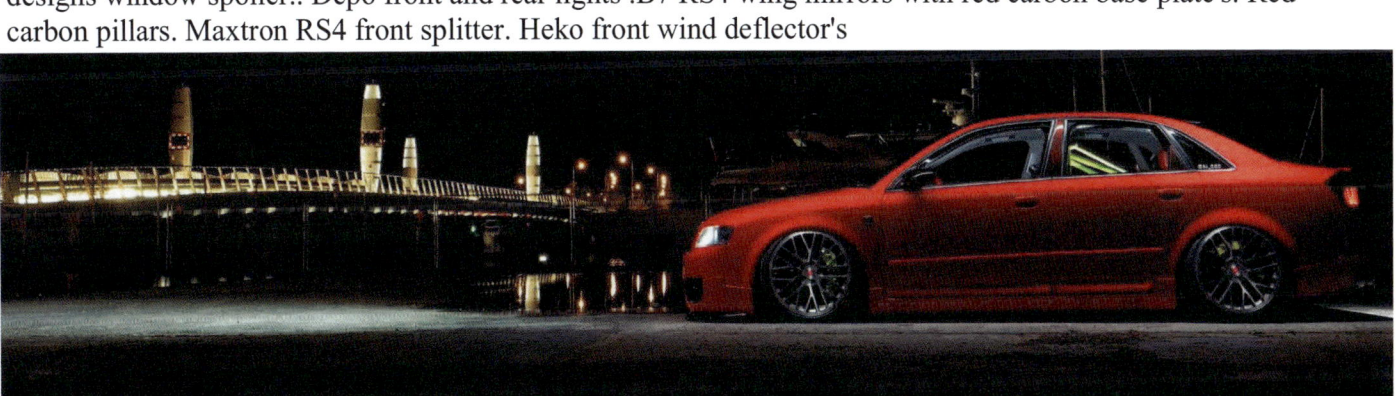

Massive Thanks to:-

@JuicydetailsUK for supporting me and being involved with totally awesome people. **Josh at Icon automotive** for helping me rebuild the engine this year. **Paddy at PMC bodyworks** for painting the car this year. Jules at @iwautomotive for supplying the 3 different sets of wheels this year. Rich at @RichardPearcephotography for always shooting the car. C6 carbon for doing all the carbon work.

Author:Paul Doherty

Kai Kriegbaum
1982 VW Golf MK1

Instagram: @illest68

My name is Kai Kriegbaum, aged 28 and come from Southern Germany. Professional, I work as a Private Client Advisor in a large Deutsche Bank.

I have been interested in cars since I was a child and I have always purchased and read many magazine's and then got to know the boy's and girl's from the '**Unique Car Society Mannheim**'. This led onto many great friendship's and a gained foothold in the scene. Through these individuals I am now part of the '**@Low Familia**' and '**@VW Home**', both are great forum's with a very close relationship.

Thanks to Corona, this year almost every car event has been cancelled otherwise, I would love to attend many events to meet good old friends and indeed get to build new friendships

The best events '**Wörthersee**', '**MIVW**', '**XS-Carnight**' and '**Tief Im Wald of Custom Junkies**'.

My car history consist of firstly driving a Skoda Fabia Combi and from here, the tuning started! After the Skoda I moved onto a Golf 6 R Static and a Passat CC which was on air ride.

Now I drive a VW Golf MK1 from 1982, I purchased it from a friend back in 2019. The car was first driven by an old lady and already had a few kilometres. It is powered by a 1.1L engine with 50PS, so I must say I drive according to the motto "Who drives slowly will be seen longer".

At the beginning of the year, I completely disassembled the car because it got a completely new paint job in the rare original colour '**Inari Silver**'. After the painting I continued with my much loved rebuild.

The Golf currently stands on some DTS Coil Over suspension with UniBall dome bearings from HK-Exclusive. At the axel turn rims from the house BBS with the designation PA514 with 195/45 R15 Nexen tyre's.

The dimensions they have are 7x15 and stand full in the wheel housing thanks to track plate's!

On the body itself, the fenders and side panels have been lightly machined to give the rims enough space and the tailgate has lost it's wiper.

You know what they say "**Kill all Wiper's!**" The bumpers are now completely black with some chrome strips instead of the original grey. On top of that, the old chrome mirrors were also used.

The interior is completely original from factory with it's brown equipment in a good and well-kept condition. So far, only a modern radio in old optics has been installed.

Over the winter the car will get a decent sound system for the trunk which is a must in everyone's life.

I terms of the work undertaken on the car, all of the work has been done by myself or with the help of friends.

I would like to give a shout out to:
'**Low Familia**' which you can find on Instagram at @low_familia.at
'**VW Home**' who are also on Instagram on @vwhome.

The pictures within his article were produced by **Sascha J** who you can find on @saschis.world.

Author: *Carla De Freitas*

Instagram: @Dazw27

Darren walker
VW Lupo 1.4 Sport

Darren walker I'm 37, from Lincoln Ex Army now a Trucker

I've always been into cars from a young age from seeing my grandad having some nice cars and my dad and uncle's, also I used to love going over the workshop and helping my dad restore old cars with his friends,

As drinking and smoking wasn't really my thing I got into cars properly and the start to modifying cars began and was around the time of the good old Max Power years which I enjoyed and made my love of cars even more and then going into the love of VW's like my Brother and has pretty much been VW ever since.

I always wanted to have a car that I built with my family and friends to be in a magazine or win at a show as that would let me know what I've created was to people's taste and to hear Woolf say my car was nice or cool and that all the hard work wouldn't of been for nothing.

The lupo started it's life as a basic car, 1.4 sport the better model lupo unless you went for the Gti which I wasn't interested in, at the time my bro had a ratty lupo and I thought it would be cool to make a real nice show car in a totally different style to his but ended up taking most the parts from him when he bought another car and built it up to what it is today with the help from my brother and friends, been to a lot of shows and won too many to count trophies it's had loads of different looks along the 7years I've owned it and 2016 was my best memorable and last year on the road winning at some of the biggest shows in the UK Edition 38, Low Collective, VW Festival and loads more with hopefully more In the future after I have rebuilt the new design,

Some of the Spec to date:-

- Full air ride suspension
- Custom boot installs
- Audi TT custom interior made to fit
- Custom rear bumper with a TT diffuser moulded into it
- 3L German Lupo conversion
- Custom 3" stainless exhaust system and manifold
- Custom vented wing
- BBS Split rims (have new custom wheels made ready for when it's back on the road)
- Have a new 1.6 engine ready to fit looking at turbo mods

The list goes on and on but I have took it off the road to rebuild it with the new engine and custom wheels I had made with a few other cheeky changes, everything done has either been done by myself or with friends as hate paying people to do stuff unless I really have to

I've always enjoyed helping friends and family with their cars or project builds in whatever way's I can and there's always something you have done that can help others or vise versa, and seeing either your own car or a friends come together and finished with a little bit of your input always puts a smile on my face and is worth the time spent.

The car scene has it's moments but 90% of the time you can make some real great long term friends from all over the world because we all enjoy the same interests, cars

Author: Andz Stinton

Tom Aspinall
1970 Plymouth Barracuda
Instagram: @tomx_asp

Hi all I'm Tom Aspinall, I'm 30, a plumber, and lover of music, drums and anything with wheels, especially if it's old.

I've been obsessed with older cars for as long as I can remember, especially late 60's to early 70's American muscle cars. The shape and style of them, the colours and the noise they make.

As a child I'd scour through the Hotwheels in supermarkets with my mum and dad trying to find them. My dad wasn't a huge fan of cars but he appreciated the cool ones, he loved his Capri back in the day.

His dad, my grandad Derick had 3 Capris through the 80's to when he died in 2014, he genuinely loved those cars.

I love the Capri too and bought and modified an '85 2.8 Injection Special to my taste over a few years. I loved how this one looked and sounded but it didn't quite scratch the itch for a big block V8 American muscle car so it was time to let it go to help fund one.

Originally it was to be part ex for the Barracuda but the day before it was being dropped to my house and the Capri taken, my mum rang and asked if she could buy the Capri and store it in my granddads garage.

She loved the car too, thought it looked great and had also driven my dads frequently when they met. My mum is now the proud owner of the 2.8 Injection Capri.

The Barracuda was delivered early in the morning and my mouth just dropped to the floor when I saw it pull up at the front of my house on the back of the low loader.

My wife Katie's eyes teared up and said it was the most beautiful thing she'd ever seen! Even the neighbours came out clapping! It can't be missed, it's a huge 1970 Plymouth Barracuda with a big block 383 (6.3ltr) V8, 727 3spd auto in the mental Sublime Lime green.

The first thing I did was fire it up and take it round the estate. The cold start is the best sound I've ever heard with the huge cam and lumpy idle through Doug's header's, it made for an interesting soundtrack at 9am on a dreary Tuesday morning in the Northwest of England.

I've always been drawn to the Chrysler E-body from 1970-74, there's something about it's low wide stance that I absolutely can't get enough of.

I love the E-body Dodge Challenger, but for me, Plymouth's Barracuda has the edge.

It came to me with brand new 17"x 9" Year One tribute wheels to the original 14" ralley wheel, they do look great and they're obviously a popular choice for these cars but they aren't the wheel I wanted to run on my Barracuda. For me, 15" is the right size wheel for a classic muscle car so the first thing I did was get in touch with North Hants Tyre's to get a set of American Racing Torque Thrust 2's in 15"x 8" but with a different offset on the rear to get the dish I wanted.

These had to be wrapped in BF Goodrich white letter tyre's as this is my favourite ever combo for wheels and tyre's, I think it looks fantastic!

Next was to be bonnet pins (or hood pins as the American's say) with the wires, I was fairly confident I could drill the 50 year old bonnet and make a half decent job of it but after some stern words from Katie, I sent it to be done by my mate at his body shop local to me. I think they look great and serve a purpose too, American cars of this era aren't renowned for their fantastic build quality and the thought of the bonnet flying up and hitting the screen made my toes curl!

Up next was a front spoiler, not the easiest thing to get hold of for this car so after trying a few first gen Camaro splitters I ordered the custom front spoiler from Spoilers By Randy in the US. They made it out of steel and got it shipped to the UK in record time! I fitted the spoiler the morning it arrived and love how it changes the front of the car.

The matte black against the madness of the Sublime Lime really works for me so a future plan is to do the front grills the same colour to tie in the back panel and front splitter.

The car has obviously had some significant engine work in the US before it came here, it is absolutely mad to drive. The way it goes from 50mph to 100 is something I've never experienced before.

The previous owner Bob Main from Scotland frequently raced this car at Santa Pod and was running high 13's just under a 100mph, very respectable for a street car and beating his stock Hemi Challenger.

The fact Bob drove this car on an 800mile round trip from Scotland to Santa Pod in Wellingborough with drag racing in between is an absolute testament as to how reliable this car is. I would drive it anywhere (depending on if I have enough cash in my pocket for fuel!) I recently drove from my home near Manchester to Santa Pod Raceway in it (around 160miles each way) and averaged 10.5 miles to the gallon!

To be honest I didn't expect much more and if you're going to be bothered about fuel mileage then a 50 year old V8 probably isn't the car for you, it is smiles per gallon after all!

I have a few more plans for this car, raise the rear a little, maybe the front driving lights that came with the high performance 'Cuda models but mostly my plans for the Barracuda is to maintain it and enjoy it! I don't believe these cars should be locked away in garage's as an investment hoping for a big return.

I find it such a shame when cars that look and sound as good as this are just locked away. Future generations need to see these cars being used and enjoyed so they can start becoming fans and enthusiasts too with a dream of owning their own one day!

The point of the muscle car was so that the average working class guy or girl can go out and enjoy cheap driving thrills without having to buy an expensive exotic Italian sports car. I think if you've got an old classic then get it out and go for a blast in it!

I really do love muscle cars of this era, not just Mopars, Camaro, Charger, Firebird, Cougar, Mustang, GTO, Challenger, RoadRunner...the list goes on, but if the Barracuda was to go then the only replacement would be a '70 Chevrolet Chevelle SS in red with black stripes....but even then it might be too tough to let the Plymouth go

One thing I'd say to anyone thinking of getting any older car for the first time though would be to forget about colour, wheels, stance, even spec...just get the most solid car you can afford. Don't be distracted by shiny paint and wide wheels with loads of dish.

Get the important bit out of the way first, go for the one with the absolute least amount of rust as this will be the costly setback in the future. I was just lucky that the one I could afford was one of my favourite colours anyway!

These cars drive like nothing else, they won't turn or stop properly (without investing in parts) they go through fuel like it's going out of fashion and finding replacement parts can sometimes be difficult but they are absolutely worth it! The noise, the power and even just sitting looking at them more than makes up for their downfalls!

My only regret with this car is not finding it sooner! It's out whenever the weather is dry, it goes to as many shows as I can get to whether it be a local meet or a huge indoor show and shine.

These cars are for enjoying and that's exactly what I do with the Barracuda.

Author: Andz Stinton

Family Friendly Group

Our group modified Mizfitz was created at the end of September 2020, in that short time we have almost reached 1000 members WOW...

We have also teamed up with 12 car related companies that have came on board to sponsor the group and have kindly offered discounts for members that are interested in using their product's or service's.

Our goals in the group is to connect with other car enthusiasts and swap and share knowledge on our pride and joys.

(MONEY PITS) We are a friendly team and don't discriminate people for what they drive

We try NOT to associate with (boy racer's) as we are family oriented group and it brings a bad name to the TRUE car enthusiasts (car scene)

In the future when covid restriction's are lifted we are going to arrange family oriented STATIC cars. Our aim in this is to come together with other car groups and meet new people/members and we also aim to raise funds for a variety of charity's.

(SCO47129)
Parent to Parent/ Peer to Peer Support Groups – 2019
Parents/carers of children, young people & adults with Additional Support Needs
(Autism, ADHD, Dyslexia & Dyspraxia)

*Our main charity we support is **differabled Scotland** which helps families with additional needs. In July this year we raised £350 at a static meet within another car group before parting and starting our own group.*

We are proud of our strong and enthusiastic team that support us on a daily basis which is done in their spare time and as a hobby

MNW-Modified Northwest

Their shows which they organise themselves are a must for any car fans, anyone with a car to show of can enter it into the show n shine events or just have it displayed.

Their group on Facebook is very well organised lot's of helpful and fun topic's, plenty of really nice people and cars.

Admin are very helpful and are very approachable, they promote a family orientated group always welcoming everyone to the fold, at events their stewards couldn't be nicer, I really enjoyed putting my car on show at Bowler's exhibition centre Trafford park, there was no lingering, they got us straight in, got us all in position, and it was a great day for all, the show and shine was won by a gorgeous mini, well worth a look.

They have a little drift exhibition, where you can be a passenger, very safe and well organised, so all in all get on this group and get your car on show.

You won't be disappointed

Group created on December 11, 2015

m.me/ModifiedNorthWest16

info@modifiednw.com

Members · 12,815

They also have a Facebook Page:

Modified North West

You can find any events they are holding advertised on this page, admin contacts, and any help you may need.

Instagram: @x.coby

Callum Roberts
Rio Yellow Honda Civic Ep2

**Hi all My name is Callum Roberts.
The reason why I drive my car is because, I have always wanted a car that would stand out from the crowd.**

I have been a fan of Honda's from a very young age! My mum owned a white Civic EG which are now quite popular builds and I was taught on Honda Motor-cross bikes therefore, I can say that Honda has been a big part of my life in that aspect!

What got me into the car scene? Well this is a funny one, as I came into the scene with a Limited Edition Vauxhall Corsa.

This meant that not many people actually liked me as no one really likes them! Still made that thing look cool though…

To be quite honest, I only started working my way up when I bought the Civic. I bought the Civic with the engine completely untouched and stock however, the car had already been lowered and Stanced which at the time, I hated! "It looked cool but impractical"

So regrettably, I sold the deep dish 17" I had on it at the time. Raised the suspension and put some black wheels on, so I could actually drive it.

Which soon quickly changed as I went back to the "stance" or "scene" look. So you could say, I somewhat reverted it back to stock then started over again.

In terms of cars stats, they are rubbish. It's an EP2 not a Type R which everyone seems to take the micky out of however, I would never do the things I have done to a EP3 as it would be a waste to drive a fast car slow.

Full Spec List:-

Painted in a sS2000 Rio yellow
Red Integra dc5 recaros
Hard race rear camber adjustable arms Bc Racing coil overs
Air walker front lip
Smoothed front bumper
Vetted steering wheel
Scroth 5 point racing harness
Boot build
Bbs lm reps 18"
3" centre pipe exhaust with 5" back box Rare clear tail lights
Side skirt extensions
Mugen rear wing
Rear wiper delete
Sun strip
Cool pikatchu sticker (favourite mod)
Mugen gear knob
Type r floor mats

When I bought the car it had been bodged. Even the exhaust was held up by cable ties when I came to change it! The front bumper was damaged badly so repaired that with fibre glass and filler. I did eventually fix car when it was drivable!

After a while I then missed how the car was when I bought it and decided to get it low and "tilty" as my mates would say, so I slowly and eventually got it back to being a show car.

In terms of work, I still have loads of planned for it. I will never get rid of it, it's so unique and most people love it and some may hate it however, most importantly, I love it!!

My dream car? Good question, I would probably say my favourite car is an Audi R8 V8 manual. It was the poster in my bedroom when I was younger and you definitely can't beat a manual.

I have only had the Civic a year, I was so excited to show this off at shows and manage to get through to some and then. This pandemic happened and all of it went down the drain! **Author: Carla De Freitas**

Joe Samondo - Toyota Camry

Instagram: @Diecastgt500
YouTube: Diecast Alive

Hi, my name is Joe Samondo I'm from Austin,TX USA and I'm a Technical Account Manager It was 2003, and 2Fast &2 Furious came out. I saw these cars, with lights underneath their cars. And the sounds of fully spooled Turbo's.

Followed by fire coming out of their exhaust! this was the time also that Need For Speed Underground came out for PS2 and PC! .

The fact that I could go into a game and customize a car the way I want it to be customized like the cars I saw in the movie 2 Fast 2 Furious. That was the day I fell in love with cars!

With that being said, my first car was a 1990 CRX. It was red, naturally aspirated black rims. lowered. It had about. 200K miles on it and it was a fun little car. But , it was a major money pit. I broke an axle on it. (I know shocker right!?) And the car just went down hill with repairs so I had to give it up.

I always was a BIG fan of naturally aspirated engines. They are harder to work on to gain power. but if done right, you can surprise people. Now a little older, and looking for my next car.

I wanted to be different. I wanted to find a car that everyone would count out. A car that was still reliable and safe with a comfortable interior for long drives. I did not want to follow the current trends.

Enter….. The Toyota Camry!

Camry's are known as grandpa cars, grocery getters.
They are meant to save gas and not increase power. To make things even more interesting, I declined to get the v6. I went with the 4 cylinder instead!

This 2.5 L 4cyl Naturally aspirated FWD Camry has a totally new redesigned engine.

The A25A-FKS engine comes with a 13:1 compression and runs on 87 octane.

This is a very complex engine as Everything on this engine is supervised by electronics!

As awesome as that sounds, what's not so awesome is pretty much, you are at a dead end when it comes to bolt-ons and tunes. But that's why I purchased this car.

I was told things like, "You should have gotten the v6." "Why waste money on a 4cyl Camry? You should have gotten a Honda!" "Don't waste your time buying parts nothing will happen." The list goes on. It's pretty funny.

This is personal to me. Because just like the Camry, I was also counted out in life.

My dad passed away when I was 14. And my mother abandoned me there after. I pretty much raised myself on my own. And learned life the hard way. I was very suicidal and actually ended up in the hospital and flat lined.

The doctors were able to revive me. I was dead for several minutes. I don't know How I am alive today. I did not go to college.

I was the poster child for going the wrong direction. However, I fought for my mind back. I got stronger, smarter, wiser. Even when no one was cheering me on and waiting for my failure, I pushed on.

Now I work for a Huge tech company, Living in one of the best cities to live in, managing Fortune 500 companies!

The path may have not been the path I wanted to go through. But I am humbled by these experiences and want to be a voice for everyone who is suffering in silence!

So that's why I got the Camry. The Camry and I are connected.

Stock, the FWD Camry comes with 206 horsepower at the crank and 186 pound-feet of torque. Not impressive numbers. Counted out. Forgotten.

The current modifications that I currently have are as follows;

AEM Cold Air Intake
Weapon R Engine Torque Damper
Non Stop Tuning Aluminium Crank Pulley
Eibach Springs
Tanabe Strut Bar
iDrive throttle control.
Air Fuel ECU Chip
falken azenis fk510 performance tires.
Asanti 20 inch wheels.
Opt 7 Under glow
Led Glow grille light.

Because of these Mods and after I dynoed the car. I am pushing 220 at the crank. 178 to the wheels! These are very impressive numbers for a 4cyl FWD Camry.

I wanted to prove to people that 4cyl Camry's can look good, gain power and have a platform for more gains!

This thing goes! Push back In your seat! Acceleration and super loud! Take the traction control off and I can burn rubber! The good news is, that now I am able to go to the grocery store a lot faster! It wasn't easy. There was a lot of frustration and even tears sometimes! I even almost sold the car! I am just being honest. It's life.

The car is not complete yet. I still am looking for a performance exhaust, headers, throttle body spacer and a 93 octane tune. Once I get all that, I would not be surprised to be hitting 300HP.

That is my goal. And I am determined as ever to get there. I can't take all the credit. I have to give A BIG BIG kudos to

Soul speed performance *for helping me with the tough installs such as the crank pulley.*

Graphics *Guys for helping me bring my wrap and decal design to life*

Tint World, *For helping me with installing the Underglow lights.*

Elysium Performance *for custom fabricating a certain part for me that I will not say as it will be a surprise and you would just need to follow my Instagram to be kept in the loop! (Sorry!)*

Author: *Carla De Freitas*

My good friend Sean Johnson who is a service advisor for round rock Nissan, but on the side gave me advice, helped with late night installs. And over all, continued to push me with great advice to make the car the way it is today!

And lastly. My Cam fam. We have a huge following. @genakamuri.

We all support each other, encourage each other. Cry with each other, coo, Joke. You name it. It is a big family that I am happy to be a part of. That's why I am writing this article. I am doing it for them! Because of all the kindness they showed to me.

It's not just my car you are featuring. It's all of us! I was able to hit many mile stones with this car. Other then the power gains. I won second place as best Toyota at the Clean Car Alliance car show in Killen, TX. A supra got 1st place. I mean c'mon! It's a Supra!

For a Camry to get second place., That was just confirmation for me. That I am heading towards the right path. This has been a very humbling experience so far, and I have met so many cool people, made wonderful connections that will last years! I am only getting started. Watch out world! This Camry is coming for YA!

Instagram @excalibur_st

Gary Miller - Fiesta ST2

My name is Gary Miller I'm 43 and I come from Bromley, Kent but I live in Great Yarmouth, and I work as a purchaser for an oil company.

I am a single dad to a great 5 yr old boy and he is the reason my passion came back for the car scene.

When I was a kid the car I had always wanted when I grew up was a MK1 Escort because my uncle had one and I just loved everything about it, the sound it made, the lines. From that day that was my dream car.

As I'm the oldest of seven kids from a single parent I never had the opportunity like a lot of people so I worked for everything I got. I left home at 17, got a job and worked hard. In 1996 when petrol was

Only 0.52p per lyric I Done a one week crash course and passed first time I then bought myself a 1982 Mk2 Fiesta 1 Ltr after six months I finally found my dream car which was a black 1973 1300 Gt MK1 Escort which I bought for £500, now this car was everything I got pulled by the cops a lot just because the car was clean and they wanted to look at it, about a year later It got written off due to a learner driver pulling out from my left on a roundabout instead of giving away to her right at 11 o'clock at night no L plates displayed nothing went to work and I got blamed for speeding as I was a young driver.

I was lucky enough to own a few more MK1 Escorts the last was painted like Cole trickle's car in days of thunder.

In 2002 moved to Norfolk with wife and daughter and lost my job and then went south as 2004 split from wife got divorced she ran up debt under my name and the only thing I had to sell worth anything was my MK1 Escort :(.

After a few years I got myself back on my feet bought a 52 plate MK6 1.4 Fiesta Zetec in Panther Black which was a great car look after so well the food garage loved working on in always serviced on time then around about 2011 and 72k miles engine packed in so traded it for a MK6 facelift 1.2ltr Fiesta which was ok but didn't really care about it.

In 2013 my flatmate who works for Ford told me that they were bringing out a new Fiesta ST and when I saw it that was it I knew I had to have it. I thought it was time I started thinking of myself.

When I finally managed to sort out my finances and sold the MK6 I bought myself a 13 plate Fiesta St180 with red seats and I loved it. In 2014 my friend at ford needed to make numbers so I traded in the white ST for yes you guessed it another white ST180 with red seats on a 64 plate.

Loved my cars but wasn't in the car scene then in 2015 I found I had a son who now lives with me then more white St's started to appear in the area then in 2017 I though I want to join a club and start going to shows with my son so we went to snetterton to a ford show I then saw a club called Kent Modified Ford so I asked if I could join as that is where the heart is, it turned out that some of the members I went to school with.

In 2018 I thought I wanted my car to be totally different from everyone and all the white St's, this is where my other passion came in handy.

Going back to being a kid I have always Been fascinated with the legend of King Arthur and the Knights of the round table, in 1981 I remember the film Excalibur done by **John Boorman** so I thought that my car would be dedicated to the film so it began.

The first thing I done was have the car mapped with Mountune MP215 along with the cat back and Exhaust by my local Ford Garage Pertwee and Back in Great Yarmouth.

I then bought the Maxton Design Front spoilers had them sprayed pearl black along with the rest of the bottom part of the car all around.

I have always Been fascinated with the legend of King Arthur and the Knights of the round table

The hardest part to do was the wrap done by @Reproart in Great Yarmouth who are a great bunch and they done a great job and not too expensive, once I found the right movie clip to go on the side and make sure it was in the correct format it came out well and as you can see well worth it then then engine bay was and again this took a while as I had to give the artist some idea's.

In the end he watched the film and once he was ready I got the engine bay parts from @paintmodz who again are a great bunch of lad's and who are really helpful and good value for money, the artist who is based in Norwich J Spurgeon.

My headlight and interior light and dials along with the new design door seals done by **SAS Conventions** on Insta and Facebook Simon and Trevor Sibthorpe, again great work and fair in price, the Ally love line kit was bought from Triple composite, all my LED bulbs bought from Autobeam.

I just rushed and got the work done in time for 2019 Fordfair would have gone to more but money and other stuff would not permit it in 2018 I went to FordFest and Ford Fair I would like to be on company stands but the waiting list it long and I tried to get sponsors without joy again was late on the scene.

Everything I have done on the car is specific to the car so you won't see another like it. My front splitter is a merge of Maxdon design due to my front spoiler and the Ally Triple composite with Fins which I had re engineered to say Excalibur.

I done some small things myself and if I needed to know I searched YouTube and found Car rambles good

In 2019 myself and my son finally went to Cornwall to Tintagel the home of King Arthur the local paper has done 2 write ups about myself and the car and of course while there it turned heads and had a lot of people asking about it.

There was loads of cameras all of a sudden appear and take photo's of my car or people standing next to it and having a photo taken with it.

I want to get some custom made wheels when I find someone who can design and make, looking for a spoiler that it different but looks right on the car.

I have a spotlight kit to install at the front, internal want to change my seat belt with @KolourKoncept a few part need paint red inside, may change the colour of my carpet to red and looking as seat design. I'm also looking at a gear knob design and centre caps for my wheels, eventually I will then may be look at engine upgrades

Check out my Online Feature for more www.stanceauto.co.uk

spec list

2014 Fiesta ST2 Frozen White BPH 215ish Top Speed they say 139MPH

Mountune MP215 and Mountune Cat Back Exhaust, Exhaust Isolators and short shift Refurbed Alloys Resprayed Spoiler, Side Skirts, Wing Mirrors Black
Sequential Indicators
Smoked LED rear lights
Wind deflectors
Maxton Design Front spoiler painted black Dark ice design gas bonnet struts
Interior lights and foot well and dashboard light changed to red
Carbon motor sports rs mk2 bonnet vents Headlight conversion
Fog conversion
Under glow
Aftermarket dials and door seals
Kenwood touch screen stereo
Part vinyl wrap
Engine bay dress up kit airbrushed and painted Door handles, centre console painted race red Cruise control Steering wheel surround painted race red Dual smoked rear led fog lights,
Gloss back bumper plastics
Maxton design abs sprint splitter painted frozen white paired with TRC Ally splitter and fins also paint frozen white, TRC ABS and Alloy side splitters with fins and rear spats also painted frozen white

Author: Andz Stinton

Alice Fairhead
1967 Volvo Amazon estate custom

My name is Alice Fairhead, I'm 21 from Bungay on the Norfolk Suffolk border.

I work at **Draganfly Motorcycles** where I've worked since I was 15 and we're the leading supplier of spares for vintage British motorcycles as well as doing my photography on the side.

I've always been into cars, my parents and grandparent have always had classic cars and motorcycles, my main influence has been my dad, he has been restoring classic cars since before I was born and is now helping me with my car, mum said she always knew when I was little (around 2 or 3 years old) if she couldn't find me, I'd be in the garage with dad - and that's still the case.

The past 3 years dads been racing his old car again and my parents and grandparents are still driving and riding classic cars and motorcycles.

The car scene is truly amazing, the people are so kind, it doesn't matter what you drive or what your problem is, someone will always help – I've gained so many of my friends from the car scene.

I drive a 1967 Volvo Amazon estate custom which I've now owned for 3 years. I saw some Amazons, saloons, at car shows we'd been to and even in stock form they really stood out to me and I really liked them. I've always loved estate cars more so I started looking for one. All classic Volvo's are rare here in the UK and that became obvious quickly.

Not long after that dad started racing competitively at Santa Pod and Shakespeare County raceway with the Volkswagen Drag Racing Club (2003-2007) which led to plenty of great weekends at the track.

It took me 2 years to find one that was in a condition I was happy with at a price I could afford. 3 years ago I was looking on the Car and Classic website and this car came up, it had been listed a while,

was in good condition although it was more than I originally planned to spend and wasn't half way round the world. So we hired a trailer and went to view it, and after a few hours later we were on our way home with it.

3 years on we've changed the front indicators, removed all side trim, smoothed off the bonnet and the tailgate, set the rear number plate into the bumper, lowered it 30mm all round and it's got wider than standard steel wheels.

We have completely changed the grille which was made from scratch (with help from dad and my partner Gregg) and for anyone wondering they are based on Morris Minor bumper over riders, they were originally made in fibreglass by dad with the pattern being donated by Gregg.

Later on we made them slightly taller and wider and sent a pattern away and I had them and cast in aluminium and powder coated like chrome

When I first got it I changed the stock single carb for a pair of SU HS6's which improved its performance a little. Fast Forward a couple of years on and I've purchased a 2.3 turbo motor and 5 speed box from a 1996 Volvo 940. Lockdown came so rather than do the work over the winter we decided to do it sooner so the stock 1800cc engine came out and sold and the new one is (sort of) in.

At the time of writing the engine is in with engine mounts made, inlet manifold is made, gearbox is in and on new mounts with gear linkage sorted and new transmission tunnel made and hydraulic clutch connected up and we're about to remove the stock back axle to swap it for a Volvo 240 axle for better gearing and better ability to take the extra power.

There's still more to do for the engine/box/trans swap but looking ahead of that I'd like to change and move the rear reflectors, radius the corners of the bonnet and respray the car, I'm thinking dark purple with some graphics on the roof. 99.9% of all work has been done by us, idea's and inspiration from close family and all fabrication work done by dad.

    Instagram: @67volvowagon
    Instagram: @af_photo_graphyy

Author: Paul Doherty

For the last few years, as a family, we've been part of a local club called the Norfolk Street Cruisers which is open to anything old and modified as well as the National Street Rod Association (@nsra_uk) and both clubs are amazing although sometimes a bad influence.

I don't think I really have a dream car I would rather have, the Volvo is something I spotted at shows and I've hunted one down and made it my own.

When at shows dad often asks me if I could take any car home with me what would it be? And to be honest most of the time I'd go home in the car I went in, sometimes we see an old 50s Chevy or Mercury custom which are really nice but I don't think I'd actually want one, that's why I've chosen to make the Volvo look like the 50s custom style, so I can have the decent Swedish built car that's also practical underneath but it still looks great on the outside.

Dave Cashmore
2001 Vauxhall Astra Bertone Convertible

Instagram: @chianticabby

Where do I start?
I've been into cars for as long as I can remember. So as soon as I was old enough, my goal was to pass my test and get a car. The first two were old bangers, then at 21 I got myself a Peugeot 309 GTi and the modifying began!

Fast forward 20 something years and a lot of cars later and here I am, still modifying cars & annoying the neighbours with a loud exhaust!

I've had this just over 3 years now and I've changed it quite a bit. A good friend of mine has one the same colour but his is an absolutely mint show car.

So every time he buys new parts, I buy his old parts! He even helps me fit them so I know it's been done properly.

What have I done to it?

It's got a genuine GSI front bumper, OPC grill & RS style bonnet vents. Blacked out side repeaters,

The rear bumper has been replaced to get rid of rear parking sensors for a smooth look & I've replaced the whole boot lid for one that had an Irmscher spoiler already on it.

It's sitting on T.A. Technix coilovers & lowered around 65mm. The wheels are 18 inch Kahn RS-C reps with 215/35/18 Kumho tyre's. The front brakes have been converted to Mk5 VXR 321mm discs & calipers.

The rears are standard but it does have M-Tech drilled & grooved discs all round with Ferodo pads.

Engine is standard apart from a derestricted air box, K&N panel filter & a cold air feed pipe from a Vectra C CDTi.

Exhaust is a Cybox stainless steel system with a straight through centre section & a pre-cat delete.

The interior has changed a fair bit too. When I got it, it had a cream leather interior. That had to go! So I swapped it out for black leather with genuine Irmscher rear headrest inserts. The clocks are now white instead of the original black ones with matching heater control surrounds.

The steering wheel is from a Zafira GSI & the centre console is a one off colour called White Silver Sparkle. The only other place you'll see that colour is in Buckingham Palace, believe it or not!

The stereo is a Pioneer head unit with Bluetooth & hands free. What's next? Upgrading all front & rear lights to LEDs, dent removal & paint correction. But why do I do it? It's not just about the car.

I've met some great people and made some good friends along the way, they know who they are.

Even made my way up to admin in **The Mad Vauxhall Club**, which I'm quite proud of. I do it because it's a way of life for me & I genuinely love it,

I love it that much i run **Max Power History** one of the biggest Facebook groups dedicated to the old Max Power Magazine.

If your in to the old style and have a car or story's to share, why not come and get involved there is 33,000 of us and your more than welcome.

Anyway, that's my story, What's yours?

Author: Paul Doherty

Instagram: @Richie1661

Richard
2012 Audi A5 S-line Cabriolet

Im Richard, 23, I live in Surrey, England, and I drive a 2012 Audi A5 S-line Cabriolet

I've been into cars my whole life, ever since I was young playing with Hot Wheels with my dad and of course we both had our favourite ones that we'd always use.

I knew what any car on the road was and had posters of cars all over my bedroom walls. Loved every Fast and Furious film and could recite the words to any Top Gear episode that was being repeated on the TV. My love for classic cars definitely came from my grandparents as they own a Triumph Herald which she's had from new.

I loved going over to stay with them for the weekend as a kid, my grandpa would always say "let's take the Triumph out for a drive" at any and every chance we got. We would just drive for the sake of driving, not to go anywhere or do anything.

For my entire working life I've been a classic and custom car upholsterer at Vamped Trimming, the perfect job for any car lover (check out our Instagram as well as mine! @vamped_trimming). From a 1-of-1 Alfa Romeo concept car; to a brand new Audi R8 and everything in between, even converting a VW split screen camper into a dog, I'm not joking, you name it and I've probably done it. I left school with terrible exam results, not wanting to go to uni. I got very lucky finding the job through a Facebook post and the rest is history.

I can remember being a kid at school when the facelift A5 range came out in 2012 and I loved it instantly, I just thought it was the most aggressive looking car on the road at the time and, in my opinion, still is today. When I eventually got fed up with my first car breaking down all the time, a heavily modded Citroen C2, I knew that was the time I could make my dream a reality.

Obviously the UK car guys know how insurance is a total killer of dream cars so that puts the RS5 well out of my reach, especially since I was 21 at the time. After looking at a few A5 coupes I eventually tried a cabriolet as they happened to have one at a dealer I was visiting.

Being able to get rid of the roof at the flick of a switch was all it took to convince me. So I found one I liked the spec of and it was mine in a matter of days. A 1.8TFSI convertible Audi was a very nice upgrade from the 1.1 Citroen I was used to driving around. Enough power to let me have some more fun and actually meant I was able to overtake those annoying slow lorries we all hate.

I think there's a few things that make my car unique and stand out but the main thing being that, to my knowledge, it's the only A5 cabriolet on air suspension in the country. I've seen countless coupes bagged but never another cabriolet.

I love that my car looks so different to other A5s on the road, the carbon fibre parts on the car are so subtle given the car is grey but they make a huge difference when compared to a standard model and could be easily missed.

I was lucky enough to find a cabriolet which didn't suffer from the common leaking roof compartment and rusting sills. Before me the car had 2 previous owners both of whom clearly looked after the car very well which made a perfect base for me to add my touches to.

The list of things I've done feels like a long one but isn't much compared to the list of things that I'd like to do with the car.

It feels like it's been a very long journey to get the car to where it is now and it's definitely an on going project.

Here's what I've done so far:

Fully polybush suspension, made a huge difference to the body roll being such a heavy car.

Bagged on Airlift Performance struts with 3P digital management and controller mounted in the ashtray.

20x10.5 Ferrada FR4 wheels with 240-30-20 tyre's stretched on to get them tucked deeper into the arches. Standard round wheel swapped out for an Audi flat bottom wheel.
Interior trims wrapped in carbon vinyl (soon to be made in real carbon).
Carbon fibre splitter.
Carbon fibre fog light trims.
Carbon fibre wing mirrors.
Carbon fibre spoiler.
Stock brakes upgrade to Brembo pads and drilled disks. Tinted windows.
Sweeping mirror indicators.

I won't be falling out of love with it any time soon given the size of the list of things that I'd like to do to the car over the coming years, a few more cosmetic things as well as some more performance mods as I've got used to the power that the car gives now.

I've been a member of many clubs over the years which has led me to meet so many great people and travel all over the place going to shows and meets.

The first club I joined, @C2UK, were the most welcoming and friendly group of people and the perfect introduction into the car community, many of whom I'm still friends with today.

Being a member of @flashcars_uk and only meeting some of them for the first time last weekend at a @b_roadhuntingclub meet has led me to write this article so I would 100% recommend joining a group and who knows where it can take you. I'm also a member of @Audiownersclubuk and have been ever since owning my A5, often going to meets and shows with them and even blasting around the country roads of Surrey for a whole day. Even meeting photographer's like @down.shift.media who took most of the pictures here.

So my car hasn't actually been Modded for all that long, a lot of the mods have been done during the lock down period as I've had so much time at home looking at the car and the Internet thinking of all the things I can change and do to it.

Because of this I haven't actually been to very many shows, the first big one I would have gone to would have been Players Classics at Goodwood which I had booked and was ready to go, but 2020 had different ideas. I can't wait for next season to start and to get to as many shows as possible.

My first car, as I've already mentioned, was a 2005 Citroen C2 1.1 which I've had since I was 17 and still have today. I did pretty much everything and anything I could do without sending my insurance through the roof. It was also bagged after spending most of it's life on coilovers it just wasn't low enough. Had 16" WCI CC10s, Corbeau bucket seats, a Retrim which of course I did myself in the brightest red I could find.

I had to remove the rear seats to fit the twin 12" 3600watt subs, which caused me to crack the windscreen at a show, in a boot build I'd made myself with 2 polished air tanks.

A custom made stainless steel exhaust and a stainless decat manifold. Eventually I bought another C2, a vts with a 1.6 engine and swapped the engines over. Of course being a French car it broke every weekend and eventually enough was enough and i got the Audi.

I don't think any car person can say they have one dream car but here's the closest I can get. My dream Jap car would have to be a Mazda RX7 which I considered getting when looking for A5's, and my dream super car is the McLaren 720S and I really hope that one day I'll see my A5 parked next to both of these in my garage, but for now I'll keep dreaming.

I hope you've enjoyed hearing about me and my car, please do check out my Instagram to see what else is coming for the A5 as well as my work @vamped_trimming.

Author: Paul Doherty

Photographer @down.shift.media

STEALTH Automotive

STEALTH AUTOMOTIVE, THE HOME OF EVERYTHING STEALTH.

Vauxhall Nova 1.2L saloon
George Rushby

Hi I'm George Rushby, I'm 18 years old and from Flitwick, Bedfordshire and work as an apprentice technician at Mercedes Benz Bedford

The Vauxhall Nova represented the first attempt by General Motors' European operation to launch a super mini - and a very successful one it was too. The little car (called the 'Opel Corsa' on the continent) had basic yet classic 3-box styling but was bang up to date underneath that legendary bodywork.

There was a vast range of trim levels and engines, as Vauxhall attempted to create the perfect Nova for just about everyone.

I have always loved the car scene mostly being a big fan of crazy modded cars and also the long projects like my nova.

*I am in the **Vauxhall nova owners club** as it is a nova. Also I am in the **Mad Vauxhall club** that holds events near me which is a great opportunity for the car to show off to the newer cars and also to make good friends around me.*

So my car is a 1989 nova saloon currently sitting on viair air suspension fitted by JD air, Japan racing minilites and has recently had a full respray.

I have owned this car for 3 year's and it is only getting better.

It recently went to Sharnbrook in Bedford for the mad Vauxhall show and cone joint second for best in show. It started from a run down rust bucket and is now gleaming in it's red paint.

This car is unique from the others as it has had heart and soul from all of my friends around me that have helped put this car to where it is now.

It is nearly finished now just got to finish the boot build, bigger engine to come and spray in the boot and under the bonnet.

And then it's on to getting more trophies and winning a hell of a lot more. These projects are not for the faint hearted; they need time and money to get them to where they want to be

If you have a Modified, Classic, Hi-Spec or just a down right Awesome looking car and you would like to Feature it in our Magazine, then get in touch with us, we have a Facebook Group dedicated to finding all the awesome cars from around the world so we can feature you and your story in the Magazine for the world to read and share,
so don't hesitate get in touch with us today!!

www.stanceauto.co.uk
@stanceautomag

Author: Paul Doherty

Martin & Luisa Knight
Bagged Audi RS3

NOVEMBER 2021

W#	MONDAY	TUESDAY	WEDNESDAY	THURSDAY	FRIDAY	SATURDAY	SUNDAY
44	1 Magazine Release day	2	3	4	5 Guy Fawkes Day	6	7
45	8	9	10	11	12	13	14
46	15	16	17	18	19	20	21
47	22	23	24	25	26	27	28
48	29	30 St. Andrew's Day (SCT) Competition Ends					

Printed in Poland
by Amazon Fulfillment
Poland Sp. z o.o., Wrocław